A Text Book Of

PRINCIPLES OF PROGRAMMING AND ALGORITHMS

For
BCA Semester - I (Course Code: 103)
As Per Savitribai Phule Pune University's Revised Syllabus
Effective from June 2013

Rajesh S. Yemul
B.E. (Comp.) MISTE
Lecturer in Computer Department,
Sou. Venutai Chavan Polytechnic,
Vadgaon (Bk.) Pune.

Abhijeet D. Mankar
M.C.S.
Lecturer,
Department of Computer Science,
Tuljaram Chaturchand College,
Baramati.

Mrs. Bhavana Chaudhary
M.Sc. (Phy.), C-DAC
Former Lecturer in Computer Science Department,
T. J. College,
Pune.

NIRALI PRAKASHAN
ADVANCEMENT OF KNOWLEDGE

N2923

Principles of Programming & Algorithms　　　　　　　　　　ISBN 978-93-83073-58-0

Third Edition : July 2015
© : Authors

The text of this publication, or any part thereof, should not be reproduced or transmitted in any form or stored in any computer storage system or device for distribution including photocopy, recording, taping or information retrieval system or reproduced on any disc, tape, perforated media or other information storage device etc., without the written permission of Authors with whom the rights are reserved. Breach of this condition is liable for legal action.

Every effort has been made to avoid errors or omissions in this publication. In spite of this, errors may have crept in. Any mistake, error or discrepancy so noted and shall be brought to our notice shall be taken care of in the next edition. It is notified that neither the publisher nor the authors or seller shall be responsible for any damage or loss of action to any one, of any kind, in any manner, therefrom.

Published By :　　　　　　　　　　　　　　　　　　　　　　　　　**Printed By :**
NIRALI PRAKASHAN　　　　　　　　　　　　　　　Repro Knowledgecast Limited,
Abhyudaya Pragati, 1312, Shivaji Nagar,　　　　　　　　　　　　　　　　　Thane
Off J.M. Road, Pune – 411005
Tel - (020) 25512336/37/39, Fax - (020) 25511379
Email : niralipune@pragationline.com

☞ DISTRIBUTION CENTRES

PUNE
Nirali Prakashan : 119, Budhwar Peth, Jogeshwari Mandir Lane, Pune 411002, Maharashtra
Tel : (020) 2445 2044, 66022708, Fax : (020) 2445 1538
Email : bookorder@pragationline.com, niralilocal@pragationline.com
Nirali Prakashan : S. No. 28/27, Dhyari, Near Pari Company, Pune 411041
Tel : (020) 24690204 Fax : (020) 24690316
Email : dhyari@pragationline.com, bookorder@pragationline.com

MUMBAI
Nirali Prakashan : 385, S.V.P. Road, Rasdhara Co-op. Hsg. Society Ltd.,
Girgaum, Mumbai 400004, Maharashtra
Tel : (022) 2385 6339 / 2386 9976, Fax : (022) 2386 9976
Email : niralimumbai@pragationline.com

☞ DISTRIBUTION BRANCHES

JALGAON
Nirali Prakashan : 34, V. V. Golani Market, Navi Peth, Jalgaon 425001,
Maharashtra, Tel : (0257) 222 0395, Mob : 94234 91860

KOLHAPUR
Nirali Prakashan : New Mahadvar Road, Kedar Plaza, 1st Floor Opp. IDBI Bank
Kolhapur 416 012, Maharashtra. Mob : 9850046155

NAGPUR
Pratibha Book Distributors : Above Maratha Mandir, Shop No. 3, First Floor,
Rani Jhanshi Square, Sitabuldi, Nagpur 440012, Maharashtra
Tel : (0712) 254 7129

DELHI
Nirali Prakashan : 4593/21, Basement, Aggarwal Lane 15, Ansari Road, Daryaganj
Near Times of India Building, New Delhi 110002
Mob : 08505972553

BENGALURU
Pragati Book House : House No. 1, Sanjeevappa Lane, Avenue Road Cross,
Opp. Rice Church, Bengaluru – 560002.
Tel : (080) 64513344, 64513355,Mob : 9880582331, 9845021552
Email:bharatsavla@yahoo.com

CHENNAI
Pragati Books : 9/1, Montieth Road, Behind Taas Mahal, Egmore,
Chennai 600008 Tamil Nadu, Tel : (044) 6518 3535,
Mob : 94440 01782 / 98450 21552 / 98805 82331,
Email : bharatsavla@yahoo.com

niralipune@pragationline.com | www.pragationline.com
Also find us on www.facebook.com/niralibooks

Preface ...

We have great pleasure in presenting a book on the subject **'Principles of Programming and Algorithms'**. This book is targeted towards the students of BCA, Semester I.

There are a number of reference books available on this topic none of them are streamlined to meet the requirement of the syllabus of Savitribai Phule Pune University for BCA course. This book is an attempt to cover most of the topics in the syllabus, which otherwise the student would have to refer to different books for different topics.

This book will help the students to get an overall view of all the topics and it is problem and solution oriented book which will definitely help them from exam point of view.

A special word of thanks to **Shri. Dineshbhai Furia, Shri. Jignesh Furia** for showing full faith in us to write this book. We also thanks to all staff members of M/s Nirali Prakashan for their excellent co-operation.

Finally, we must thank our family members for their constant encouragement without which this book would not have been possible.

AUTHORS

Syllabus ...

1. Introduction [5]

    1.1   Concept: Problem Solving, Algorithm

    1.2   Program development Cycle

    1.3   Characteristics of an Algorithm

    1.4   Time Complexity: Big-Oh Notation

    1.5   Flowcharts

    1.6 Simple Examples: Algorithms and flowcharts

2. Simple Arithmetic Problems [13]

    2.1   Addition / Multiplication of Integers

    2.2   Determining if a Number is +ve / –ve / Even / Odd

    2.3   Maximum of 2 Numbers, 3 Numbers

    2.4   Sum of First n Numbers, given n Numbers

    2.5   Integer Division, Digit Reversing, Table Generation for n, ab

    2.6   Factorial, Sine Series, Cosine Series, nCr, Pascal Triangle

    2.7   Prime Number, Factors of a Number

    2.8   Other Problems such as Perfect Number, GCD of 2 Numbers etc.

    (Write Algorithms and Draw Flowcharts)

3. Recursion [8]

    3.1   Concept

    3.2   Multiplication

    3.3   Factorial

    3.4   Ackerman function

    3.5   Fibonacci series

    3.6   Permutation Generation

4. Algorithms using Arrays [8]

    4.1   Maximum and Minimum of Array, Reversing Elements of an Array

    4.2   Mean and Median of n Numbers

    4.3   Row Major and Column Major Form of Array Representation

    4.4   Matrices: Addition, Multiplication, Transpose, Symmetry, Upper/Lower Triangular

5. Sorting and Searching [13]

    5.1   Insertion sort

    5.2   Bubble sort

    5.3   Selection Sort

    5.4   Quick sort (Recursive)

    5.5   Merge Sort

    5.6   Radix Sort

    5.7   Bucket Sort

    5.8   Counting Sort

    5.9   Sequential and Binary search

    (Performance Analysis for space requirement and speed using Big-Oh notation is essential)

***

Contents ...

1. **Introduction to Problem Solving**   1.1 – 1.60

2. **Simple Arithmetic Problems**   2.1 – 2.30

3. **Recursion**   3.1 – 3.14

4. **Algorithms Using Arrays**   4.1 – 4.36

5. **Sorting and Searching**   5.1 – 5.36

***

Chapter 1...

Introduction to Problem Solving

Contents ...

- 1.1 Concept
    - 1.1.1 Definition of Problem
    - 1.1.2 Problem Solving
        - 1.1.2.1 Definition
        - 1.1.2.2 Problem Solving Steps
        - 1.1.2.3 Problem Solving Techniques
- 1.2 Program Development Cycle
- 1.3 Algorithms
    - 1.3.1 Definition
    - 1.3.2 Characteristics
    - 1.3.3 Types of Algorithms
    - 1.3.4 Advantages and Disadvantages
- 1.4 Flowcharts
    - 1.4.1 Definition
    - 1.4.2 Flowcharting Symbols
    - 1.4.3 Advantages
    - 1.4.4 Limitations
- 1.5 Algorithm Complexities
    - 1.5.1 What is Complexity?
    - 1.5.2 Time Complexity
    - 1.5.3 Space Complexity
    - 1.5.4 Big 'O' Notation
- 1.6 Examples of Algorithms and Flowcharts
- • Questions
- • University Questions and Answers

1.1 Concept

- A problem is any situation in which you have a starting point, a set of directions, and the need to create a solution or answer.
- A problem is a situation that confronts someone, that requires solution, and for which the path to the solution is not immediately known.
- A problem is a question or situation that motivates you to search for a solution. This implies first that you want or need to solve the problem and second that you have to search for a way to find a solution. Whether a question is a problem or an exercise depends on the prior knowledge of the problem solver.
- Specifically, the task of defining the problem consists of identifying what it is you know (input-given data), and what it is you want to obtain (output-the result).

Two aspect of problem:

1. The detective for dealing with the crisis and the analytical parts of problem definition, and
2. The explorer for dealing with the context and the opportunity aspects of the problem.

- Problem solving is a process of finding a solution for a particular problem.

1.1.1 Definition of Problem

- We can define problem as "a state of desire for reaching a definite goal from a present condition".

OR

- "A problem is an issue or obstacle which makes it difficult to achieve a desired goal, objective or purpose".

OR

- "Problem refers to a situation, condition or issue that is yet unresolved".

OR

- A problem is "a question or situation raised for consideration or solution".

1.1.2 Problem Solving

- Problem solving is the sequential process of analyzing information related to a given situation and generating appropriate response options.
- The ultimate goal of problem-solving is to overcome obstacles and find a solution that best resolves the issue.
- There are a number of different mental process at work during problem-solving. These include:
    1. Perceptually recognizing a problem.
    2. Representing the problem in memory.

3. Considering relevant information that applies to the current problem.
4. Identify different aspects of the problem.
5. Labeling and describing the problem.

1.1.2.1 Definition

- Problem solving is "the process of working through details of a problem to reach a solution".

OR

- Problem-solving is a mental process that involves discovering, analyzing and solving problems.
- Problem solving is a thinking process includes:
    1. Understand the problem (communication and analysis).
    2. Plan a solution (modeling and design).
    3. Carry out the plan (code generation).
    4. Examine the result for accuracy (testing and quality assurance).
- Fig. 1.1 has a single main module, with which we associate a level number of 1, which gives the brief general description of the system. The main module refers to a number of subordinate modules which have been numbered as level 2, 3, 4 respectively.

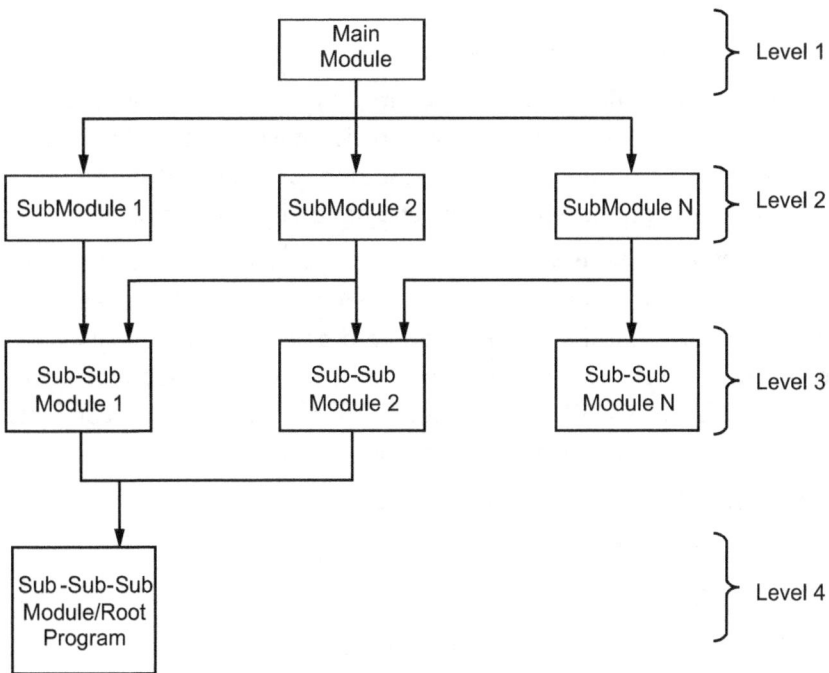

Fig. 1.1: Levels of problem solving

1.1.2.2 Problem Solving Steps

- Generally there are five widely accepted steps in the problem solving process as shown in Fig. 1.2.

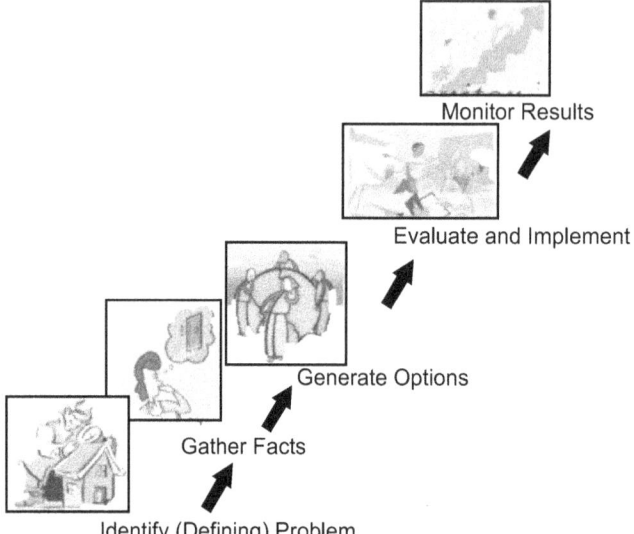

Fig. 1.2

- Problem solving steps are described below:

    1. **Defining (identifying) the problem:** In almost every problem solving methodology the first step is defining or identifying the problem. It is the most difficult and the most important of all the steps. It involves diagnosing the situation so that the focus on the real problem and not on its symptoms.

        Defining the solution: We often think of "solving a problem" in the sense of making it go away, so that the problem no longer exists. This indeed is one kind of solution, but it is not the only kind. Some problems cannot be eliminated entirely: we are never likely to eliminate trash, or the wear on automobile tires, or the occurrence of illness. We can, however, create solutions or treatments that will make each of these problems less harmful.

    2. **Gather facts:** Some means of gathering data are:
        (i) Define key terms.
        (ii) Articulate assumptions.
        (iii) Discuss the problem with someone else.
        (iv) Get the viewpoint of others.

3. **Generate alternate options:** One way to identify potential solutions is to represent the problem either internally or externally. By representing the problem, you will select information that is relevant including the goal, the initial state, the operators and restrictions. Operators are actions that change the initial state of the problem into another. Then you may categorize it as a type of problem, develop similar situations, identify the criteria for evaluating the solution and adjust and combine ideas. Some of the tools used are:

   (i) Systematic trial and error.

   (ii) Proximity searching.

   (iii) Means ends.

   (iv) Fractional method.

   (v) Knowledge based.

4. **Implement and Evaluate:** Make a list of the different options that you have generated. Select one or more solutions options from near the top of your list to try. Does the solution meet the goals and conditions set by the problem? Frequently the better option for implementation is the number two or number three choice. Measure the impact of the solution. The evaluation of your implementation is not based on whether or not you followed the steps, but on whether or not your goals are met.

5. **Monitor the solution:** Re-apply measurements to confirm that change has taken place.

   (i) Check to ensure that the changes do not negatively impact another area.

   (ii) Provide sufficient information and training so that change can take place and be sustained.

   (iii) Reflect on the problem solving process used. What would you have done differently.

1.1.2.3 Problem Solving Techniques (Oct. 2014)

- There are many approaches to problem solving, depending on the nature of the problem and the people involved in the problem.
- Fig. 1.3 shows various problem solving techniques.

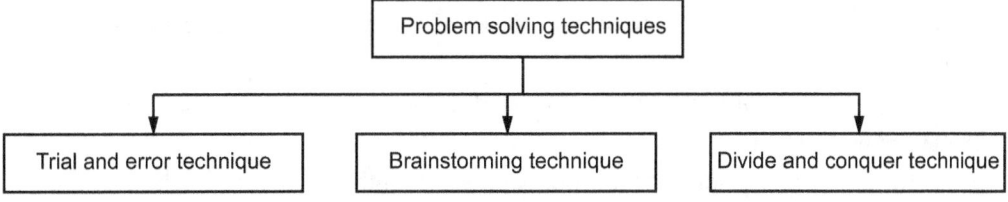

Fig. 1.3

(I) Trial and Error Method (Technique):

- Trial and error, or trial by error, is a general method of problem solving for obtaining knowledge, both propositional knowledge and know-how.
- In the field of computer science, the method is called "generate and test". Trial and Error approach is more successful with simple problems.
- Trial and Error approach can be seen as one of the two basic approaches to problem solving and is contrasted with an approach using insight and theory.
- A trial and error approach to problem solving involves trying a number of different solutions and ruling out those that do not work.
- This approach can be a good option if you have a very limited number of options available.
- This method is often used by people who have little knowledge in the problem area.

Features of Trial and Error Method:

1. **Solution-oriented:** Trial and error makes no attempt to discover why a solution works, merely that it is a solution.
2. **Problem-specific:** Trial and error makes no attempt to generalize a solution to other problems.
3. **Non-optimal:** Trial and error is an attempt to find a solution, not all solutions, and not the best solution.
4. **Needs little knowledge:** Trial and error can proceed where there is little or no knowledge of the subject.

Advantages:

1. Easy to implement.
2. This method is best in situations where you have more test subjects.

Disadvantage:

1. Time consuming because of need to run each and every test.

(II) Brainstorming Method (Technique):

- Brainstorming is a group creativity technique designed to generate a large number of ideas for the solution to a problem.
- Brainstorming is problem solving technique that uses a group of people to solve a problem.
- Purpose of a brainstorming session is to work as a group to define a problem and find a plan of action to solve it.
- Brainstorming process involves a group working together and stating ideas, arguing the merits of those ideas, supplementing those ideas or rejecting those ideas.

- Brainstorming is often seen in the workplace, when a work group meets to consider and create multiple ideas.
- It is a method of shared problem solving in which all members of a group spontaneously contribute ideas for solution of a problem.
- Brainstorming is where a group of people put social inhibitions and rules aside with the aim of generating new ideas and solutions.

Approach of Brainstorming: There are four basic rules in brainstorming.

1. **Combine and Improve ideas** approach is assumed to lead to better and more complete ideas than merely generating new ideas alone. It is believed to stimulate the building of ideas by a process of association.

2. **No criticism** is often emphasized that in group brainstorming, criticism should be put on hold. Instead of immediately stating what might be wrong with an idea, the participants focus on extending or adding to it, reserving criticism for a later critical stage of the process. By suspending judgment, one creates a supportive atmosphere where participants feel free to generate unusual ideas.

3. **Focus on quantity** rule is a means of enhancing divergent production, aiming to facilitate problem solving through the maximum quantity breeds quality. The assumption is that the greater the number of ideas generated, the greater the chance of producing a radical and effective solution.

4. **Unusual ideas are welcome:** To get a good and long list of ideas, unusual ideas are welcomed. They may open new ways of thinking and provide better solutions than regular ideas. They can be generated by looking from another perspective or setting aside assumptions.

Variations of Brainstorming Techniques:

1. **Nominal group technique:** The nominal group technique is a type of brainstorming that encourages all participants to have an equal say in the process. It is also used to generate a ranked list of ideas. Participants are asked to write down their ideas anonymously. Then the moderator collects the ideas and each is voted on by the group.

2. **Group passing technique:** Each person in a circular group writes down one idea, and then passes the piece of paper to the next person in a clockwise direction, who adds some thoughts. This is repeated until everybody gets their original piece of paper back. By this time, it is likely that the group will have extensively elaborated each idea.

3. **Team idea mapping method:** Team idea mapping method of brainstorming works by the method of association. It may improve collaboration and increase the quantity of ideas, and is designed so that all attendees participate and no ideas are rejected.

4. **Electronic brainstorming:** Electronic brainstorming is a computerized version of the manual brainwriting (brain storming) technique. It can be done via e-mail. Electronic brainstorming also enables much larger groups to brainstorm on a topic than would normally be productive in a traditional brainstorming session. Electronic brainstorming eliminates many of the problems of standard brainstorming, such as production blocking and evaluation apprehension.

5. **Directed brainstorming:** Directed brainstorming is a variation on electronic brainstorming (brainwriting) described above. It can be done manually or with computer technology. Directed brainstorming works when the solution space is known prior to the session. If known, that criteria can be used to intentionally constrain the ideation, process. In directed brainstorming, each participant is given one sheet of paper and told the brainstorming question.

6. **Individual brainstorming:** Individual Brainstorming is the use of brainstorming on a solitary basis. Individual brainstorming typically includes such techniques as free writing, free speaking, word association, and the spider web, which is a visual note taking technique in which a people diagram their thoughts.

Advantages of Brainstorming:
1. Easy to understand i.e. it is not a complicated technique.
2. It is inexpensive.
3. If controlled properly it is a quick way of generating ideas.
4. Encourages creative thinking and thinking "out of the box".
5. Generates ideas and solutions that can be used elsewhere.
6. Provides an opportunity for widespread participation and involvement.

Disadvantages of Brainstorming:
1. As this is a group activity, participants have to listen patiently and have to spend more time by sharing their ideas till they are noticed by others.
2. More discrete or introvert participants might find it difficult to express their crazy or unorthodox ideas.

(III) Divide and Conquer Method (Technique):
- The name divide and conquer is because the problem is conquered by dividing it into several smaller problems.
- Divide and conquer is an approach to solving a problem that is a special case of means-ends analysis.
- In divide and conquer, one solves a problem by first defining a subgoal that involves solving a smaller version of the same kind of problem.
- In other words, divide and conquer is the explicit use of recursion to solve a problem.

- The divide-and-conquer strategy solves a problem by:
    1. Breaking it into sub problems that are themselves smaller instances of the same type of problem.
    2. Solving these subproblems independently.
    3. Appropriately combining their answers.

Working:

- It works by recursively breaking down a problem into two or more sub-problems of the same (or related) type, until these become simple enough to be solved directly.
- The solutions to the sub-problems are then combined to give a solution to the original problem.
- A Divide and Conquer algorithm is closely tied to a type of recurrence relation between functions of the data in question; data is divided into smaller portions and then result is calculated.
- Divide and Conquer technique is the basis of efficient algorithms for all kinds of problems, such as sorting (quick sort, merge sort) and the discrete Fast Fourier Transforms (FFTs). Its application to numerical algorithms is commonly known as binary splitting.

Advantages of Divide and Conquer Technique:

1. **Solving difficult problems:** Divide and conquer is a powerful tool for solving conceptually difficult problems, all it requires is a way of breaking the problem into sub-problems, of solving the trivial cases and of combining sub-problems to the original problem.
2. **Algorithm efficiency:** The divide-and-conquer paradigm often helps in the discovery of efficient algorithms.
3. **Parallelism:** Divide and conquer algorithms are naturally adapted for execution in multi-processor machines, especially shared-memory systems where the communication of data between processors does not need to be planned in advance, because distinct sub-problems can be executed on different processors.
4. **Memory access:** Divide-and-conquer algorithms naturally tend to make efficient use of memory caches. The reason is that once a sub-problem is small enough, it and all its sub-problems can, in principle, be solved within the cache, without accessing the slower main memory.

Disadvantages of Divide and Conquer Technique:

1. **Slow Recursion:** The overhead of the repeated subroutine calls, alongwith that of storing the call stack, can outweigh any advantages of the approach. This, however, depends upon the implementation style: with large enough recursive base cases, the overhead of recursion can become negligible for many problems.

2. **Complicated for simple problems:** Another problem of a divide and conquer approach is that, for simple problems, it may be more complicated than an iterative approach, especially if large base cases are to be implemented for performance reasons.

1.2 Program Development Cycle   (Oct. 2014, April 2015)

- Program development cycle is a set of phases and steps that are followed by problem solver to define, develop and maintain a program.
- Planning your program using a sequence of steps, referred to as the program development cycle.
- Fig. 1.4 shows program development cycle.

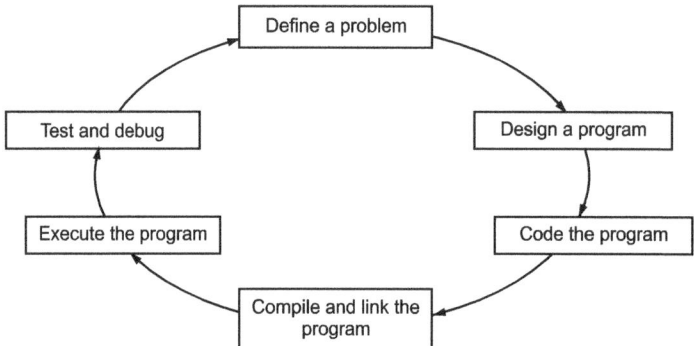

Fig. 1.4: Program development cycle

- The program development cycle involves following steps:

Step 1: Define the Problem

- It is very important that you understand the problem you are trying to solve. Make sure you read the problem specifications carefully.
- Know what data is to be input into the program and what form that data should be in. Also, know what processing has to be done to that data.
- Finally, determine what the expected output is supposed to be and what form the output must take.

Step 2: Design the Program

- There are several ways of describing program design. Two common methods are by flowcharts and pseudocode.
- A flowchart is a graphic description of a program design that uses combinations of various standard flowchart symbols.
- We shall use flowcharts to represent only the basic program control structures. Pseudocode (literally, "false code") describes program design using English. Pseudocode avoids the syntax of a programming language and, instead, emphasizes the design of the problem solution.

Step 3: Code the Program

- To code a program means to translate the design from step 2 into a computer programming language.
- Code the program by entering it into your IDE's text editor, or any text editor on your computer system. Make sure that you save the program to disk before proceeding to the next step.
- In the next step of the program development cycle, you will submit the program code, called the source program or the source code, to the computer for compilation.

Step 4: Compile and Link the Program

- The only language a given computer understands is its own machine language. A machine language instruction is a binary-coded instruction (consisting of zeros and ones) that commands the computer to do one specific task, such as add 1 to a register.
- Each computer has its own machine language. The machine language for a Sun workstation is different from the machine language of a Macintosh, which is different from the machine language of an IBM PC, and so on. Because machine language is in binary, it is difficult to write and find errors in machine language programs.
- Because a computer understands only its own machine language, it cannot execute high-level or middle-level language instructions directly. The computer, using a program called a compiler, must translate middle-level and high-level language programs into equivalent machine language programs. A compiler is a specialist. It translates only one high-level or middle-level language into a specific machine language.
- A compiler has two main functions.
  - (i) Checking fatal syntax errors.
  - (ii) Translate the code into machine specific language.
- First it checks the source program for syntax errors. Syntax errors are errors in the grammar of the programming language. If there are any fatal syntax errors (that is, errors so severe that the compiler does not understand the statement and cannot translate the statement into machine language), the compiler will stop and notify you of the errors it found.
- If the compiler finds no fatal errors, it translates each high-level language instruction into one or more machine language instructions. This machine language version of the source program is the object program.

Step 5: Execute the Program

- Once you have compiled and linked the program, you are ready to execute the program.
- Executing the program is usually quite simple. In some IDEs, all you need to do is select the execute option from a menu or click an icon.

Step 6: Test and Debug the Program
- Even if a program executes, it does not mean that the program is correct.
- Even if a program gives correct results using some data, it does not mean that the program will give correct results using another set of data.
- Thus, program should be tested for various possible sets of data and should be debugged whenever required.

1.3 Algorithms (Oct. 2014, April 2015)

- An algorithm is a finite set of precise instructions for performing a computation or for solving a problem.
- Algorithm is a sequence of activities to be processed for getting desired output (solution) from a given input (problem).
- An algorithm can be thought of as the detailed instructions for carrying out some operation. A computer program has to follow a sequence of exact instructions to accomplish this. This sequence of instructions is called an algorithm.

Uses of Algorithm:
1. Using the algorithms basic layout the program can be developed in any desired language.
2. An algorithm is a representation in simple English language so it is very easy to understand, so problem can be easily and simply solved.
3. Algorithm facilitates easy coding.

Approaches for Designing an Algorithm:
1. **Top-down Approach:** A top-down design approach starts by identifying the major components of the system or program decomposing them into their lower level components and iterating until the desired level of module complexity is achieved. In this we start with the topmost module and incrementally add modules that it calls, (For example: 'C' language).
2. **Bottom-up Approach:** A bottom-up design approach starts with designing the most basic or primitive components and proceeds to higher level components. Starting from the very bottom, the operations that provide a layer of abstraction are implemented.

- Various algorithmic strategies can be written using two methods.
    1. **Recursive Algorithm:** A Recursive algorithm is an algorithm which calls itself with smaller (or simple) input values, and which obtains the result for the current input by applying the same operations for the smaller (or simpler) input. More generally if a problem can be solved utilizing solutions to smaller versions of the same problem, and the smaller versions reduce to easily solvable cases, then one can use a recursive algorithm to solve the problem.
    2. **Iterative Algorithm:** In these algorithms, the process is carried out repetitively on the inputs in order to achieve the desired output.

1.3.1 Definition

- We can define algorithm as "a set of instructions for solving a problem".

OR

- A step-by-step procedure for solving a particular problem is an Algorithm.

OR

- An algorithm can be defined as "a process that performs some sequence of operations in order to solve a given problem".

OR

- An algorithm is "a step-by-step solution to a problem".

1.3.2 Characteristics   (Oct. 2014)

- Every algorithm must satisfy the following characteristics:

    1. **Input**   : An algorithm must have zero or more quantities, (data) as input which are externally supplied.
    2. **Output**   : After processing the statements in an algorithm step-by-step, statement will generate some result. Hence, atleast one output must be produced.
    3. **Definiteness**   : Each instruction must be clear and distinct.
    4. **Finiteness**   : The algorithm must terminate after a finite number of steps.
    5. **Effectiveness** : Each operation must be definite also it should be feasible i.e. practically it should be possible.

1.3.3 Types of Algorithms

- The various types of algorithms are Brute force, Divide-and-conquer, Greedy algorithm and Backtracking.

1. **Brute force algorithm:**

- These are algorithms that use obvious non-sophisticated approaches to solve the problems in hand.
- Typically, they are useful for small domains, due to large overheads in sophisticated approaches. Examples are:

    (i) Bubble sort.

    (ii) Computing the sum of N numbers by direct addition.

    (iii) Standard matrix multiplication.

    (iv) Linear (sequential) search.

2. Divide and Conquer algorithm:

- Perhaps the most famous algorithmic paradigm, Divide-and-Conquer is based on partitioning the problem into two or more smaller sub-programs, solving them (using recursion or if they are simple enough, directly) and combining the sub-problem solutions into a solution for the original problem.

- Example of D and C algorithms includes:

    (i) Merge Sort and Quick sort.

    (ii) The Fast Fourier Transform.

    (iii) Strassen's Matrix Multiplication.

3. Greedy algorithms:

- Greedy algorithms always make the choice that seems best at the moment. This locally optimal choice is made with the hope that it leads to a globally optimal solution.

- Some greedy algorithms may not be guaranteed to always produce an optimal solution. Greedy algorithms are often applied to combinational optimization problems.

- Example of Greedy algorithms include:

    (i) Kruskal's and Prim's minimal spanning tree algorithms.

    (ii) Dijsktra's single source shortest path algorithm.

    (iii) Huffman Coding.

4. Backtracking algorithm:

- Backtracking is used to solve problems in which a sequence of objects is selected from a specified set or a sequence of decisions is made within a specified set of constraints so that the sequence satisfies some criterion. Often the goal is to find any feasible solution rather than an optimal solution.

- Examples include:

    (i) Depth First Search.

    (ii) 8 Queens problem.

    (iii) Traveling salesperson problem.

1.3.4 Advantages and Disadvantages   (April 2015)

Advantages: (April 2015)

1. An algorithm gives a language independent layout of the program.
2. It is step-by-step procedure of a solution to a given problem, which is very easy and simple to understand.
3. It has got a definite procedure.

4. It is easy to first develop an algorithm and then convert it into a flowchart and then into a computer program.
5. It is easy to debug as every step is got its own logical sequence.

Disadvantages: (April 2015)
1. It is time consuming.
2. It is cumbersome, as an algorithm is developed first which is converted into flowchart and then into a computer program.

1.4 Flowcharts (April 2015)

- A solution of every problem should be planned in a effective manner a step-by-step format. This planning can be symbolically represented with the use of flowcharts.
- A flowchart is a graphical representation of a program flow or an algorithm of a problem to be solved.
- Flowchart is an important tool which is used by programmers and analysts for tracing the information flow and the logical sequence for data processing.
- A flowchart is a diagrammatic representation that illustrates the sequence of operations to be performed to get the solution of a problem.
- A flowchart describes what operations (and in what sequence) are required to solve a given problem.
- Flowcharts are used in analyzing, designing, documenting or managing a process or program in various fields.
- The purpose of flowchart to show flow are sequence of operation or steps to be performed to get a solution of problem.

Principles of Flowcharting:
1. Pictorial representation of flowchart makes it a convenient method of communication.
2. It promotes logical accuracy and is a key to correct programming.
3. It takes care that no path is left incomplete without any action being taken.
4. It helps to develop program logic and serves as documentation.
5. It is an important tool for planning and designing a new system.

- Computer professional use following types of flowcharts:
    1. **System flowchart:** Used by system analyst. This flowchart shows various processes, subsystems, outputs and operations on data in a system.
    2. **Program flowchart:** Used by computer programmers. This flowchart shows program structure, logic flow and operations performed.

1.4.1 Definition

- We can define flowchart as "a symbolic representation of a solution to be given task problem".

OR

- "Graphical representation of a process is called as flowchart".

OR

- A flowchart is "a pictorial representation of an algorithm".

OR

- "Flowchart is "a pictorial or symbolic representation of a given problem".

1.4.2 Flowcharting Symbols   (Oct. 2014, April 2015)

- Flowcharts use special shapes to represent different types of actions or steps in a process.
- Following Table 1.1 shows different flowcharting symbols.

Table 1.1: Flowcharting symbols

Symbol	Name (alternates)	Meaning
▭	Process	An operation or action step.
⬭	Terminator	A start or stop point in a process.
◇	Decision	A question or branch in the process.
▯	Predefined process	A formally defined sub-process.
▱	Data (I/O)	Indicates data inputs and outputs (I/O) to and from process.
▭	Document	A document or report.
▭	Multi-document	Same as document but well multiple document.
⬡	Preparation	A preparation or set-up process step.
⌂	Display	A machine display.
○	Connector	A jump from one point to another.
⏷	Off-page connector	Continuation onto another page.
▽	Merge (Storage)	Merge multiprocess into one.
△	Extract	Extract a measurement.

Symbol	Name (alternates)	Meaning
⎡⎤	Stored data	Data storage symbol in flowchart.
🗄	Magnetic disk (database)	A database.
⌀	Direct access storage	Storage on a hard disk.
→	Flow Line	Indicates the direction of data flows.

1.4.3 Advantages

- The benefits (advantages) of flowcharts are as follows:
    1. **Proper Documentation:** Flowcharts serve as a good program documentation, which is needed for various purposes.
    2. **Efficient Coding:** The flowcharts act as a guide or blueprint during the systems analysis and program development phase.
    3. **Efficient Program Maintenance:** The maintenance of operating program becomes easy with the help of flowchart. It helps the programmer to put efforts more efficiently on that part.
    4. **Proper Debugging:** The flowchart helps in debugging process.
    5. **Communication:** Flowcharts are better way of communicating the logic of a system to all concerned.
    6. **Effective Analysis:** With the help of flowchart, problem can be analysed in more effective way.

1.4.4 Limitations

- The disadvantages (limitations) of flowchart are as follows:
    1. **Loss of technical details:** The essentials of what is done can easily be lost in the technical details of how it is done.
    2. **Complex logic:** Sometimes, the program logic is quite complicated. In that case, flowchart becomes complex and clumsy.
    3. **Alterations and Modifications:** If alterations are required, the flowchart may require redrawing completely.
    4. **Reproduction:** As the flowchart symbols cannot be typed, reproduction of flowchart becomes a problem.
    5. **Time consuming:** Developing and constructing a flowchart is time consuming. Flowchart requires more time to construct.

Comparison (Difference) between Algorithm and Flowchart:

Algorithm	Flowchart
1. An algorithm is just a detailed sequence of a simple steps that are needed to solve a problem.	1. A flowchart is a graphical representation of an algorithm.
2. An algorithm is a description of how to carry out a process. An algorithm lists the steps those must be followed to complete the process.	2. A flowchart consists of a sequence of instructions linked together by arrows to show the order in which the instructions must be carried out.
3. An algorithm is a precise rule (or set of rules) specifying how to solve some problem. Algorithm is stepwise analysis of the work to be done.	3. Each instruction is put into a box. The boxes are different shapes of depending upon what the instruction is.
4. Algorithm gives language independent layout of the program or problem.	4. Flowchart gives logical flow of program or problem.
5. Easy to update.	5. Difficult to update.
6. Less time required for write an algorithm.	6. Time consuming to write and draw a flowchart.

1.5 Algorithm Complexities

1.5.1 What is Complexity?

- Complexity of an algorithm is a function of size of input of a given problem instance which determines how much running time/memory space is needed by the algorithm in order to run to completion.
- Suppose M is an algorithm and n is the size of the input data. The time and space used by the algorithm M are the two main measures for the efficiency of M. The time is measured by counting the number of key operations-in sorting and searching algorithm.
- The complexity of an algorithm M is the function f(n) which gives the running time and or storage requirement of the algorithm in terms of the size n or the input data.
- Frequently the storage space required by an algorithm is simply a multiple of the data size n. It is implied that the term "complexity" shall refer to the running time of the algorithm.
- Example:
  ```
  For i = 1 to n
  Begin
  write(i)
  End
  ```

- The write statement is executed n times. The condition is checked for i from 1 to n times and condition is executed n times to get n output. The total number of statements executed will be 2n. We say that the complexity is of the order of n. The notation used is big-O i.e. O(n).
- We call them computational complexity, which is a characterization of the time or space requirements to solve a problem by a particular algorithm.
- Analysis of the program requires two main considerations one is time complexity and other is space complexity.

1.5.2 Time Complexity (Oct. 2014, April 2015)

- The time complexity of a program or algorithm is the amount of computer time that it needs to run to completion.
- To measure time complexity of an algorithm, we concentrate on developing only the frequency count for key statements.

Definition:
- Time complexity is "a measure of the amount of time required to execute an algorithm".

OR

- The time complexity of an algorithm or a program is the amount of time it needs to run to completion.

OR

- Time complexity is defined as, "the time required for the computer to run a program".
- The exact time will depend on the implementation of the algorithm, programming language, optimizing the capabilities of the compiler used, the CPU speed, other hardware characteristics/specifications and so on.
- To measure time complexity of an algorithm, we concentrate on developing only the frequency count for key statements.

    1. Algorithm A   :   a = a + 1
    2. Algorithm B   :   for x = 1 to n step 1

                             a = a + 1

                             loop
    3. Algorithm C   :   for x = 1 to n step 1

                             for y = 1 to n step 1

                             a = a + 1

                             loop

- Frequency count of algorithm A is 1. Frequency count of algorithm B is n. Frequency count of algorithm C is n^2.
- This means we will determine only those statements which may have the greatest frequency count.

1.5.3 Space Complexity (Oct. 2014)

- The space complexity of an algorithm or program is the amount of memory that it needs to run to completion.

Definition:

- Space complexity is defined as, "the amount of memory that a computer needs to run a program algorithm".

OR

- The space complexity of an algorithm is "the amount of memory required to execute to completion of a program/algorithm".

OR

- Space complexity is "the amount of computing memory space needed to execute an algorithm".

- Following are the reasons for studying space complexity:

    1. If the program is to run on multi user system, it may be required to specify the amount of memory to be allocated to the program.
    2. We may be interested to know in advance that whether sufficient memory is available to run the program.
    3. There may be several possible solutions with different space requirements.
    4. Can be used to estimate the size of the largest problem that a program can solve.

- The space needed by a program consists of following components:

    1. **Instruction space:** Space needed to store the executable version of the program and it is fixed.
    2. **Data space:** Space needed to store all constants, variable values and has further following components:
        (a) Space needed by constants and simple variables. This space is fixed.
        (b) Space needed by fixed sized structural variables, such as arrays and structures.
        (c) Dynamically allocated space: This space usually varies.
    3. **Environment stack space:** This space is needed to store the information to resume the suspended i.e. partially completed functions. Each and every time a function is invoked the following data is saved on the environment stack:
        (a) Return address i.e., from where it has to resume after completion of the called function.
        (b) Values of all lead variables and the values of formal parameters in the function being invoked.

- The space needed by the program is the sum of following requirements:
  1. **Fixed space requirement:** This includes the instruction space, for simple variables, fixed size structured variables and constants.
  2. **Variable space requirement:** These consist of space needed by structured variables whose size depends on particular instance of variables. It also includes the additional space required when the function uses recursion.

1.5.4 Big 'O' Notation (Oct. 2014)

- We can express the time complexity of a program in terms of the order of magnitude of frequency count using the Big O notation.
- If f(n) represent the computing time of some algorithm and g(n) represent a known standard function like n, n^2, n log n etc. then to write f(n) in O g(n) means that f(n) of n is equal to biggest order of function g(n).
- Big 'O' notation helps to determine the time as well as space complexity of the algorithm. Using Big 'O' notation, the time taken by the algorithm and the space required to run the algorithm can be ascertained. This information is useful to set algorithms and to develop and design efficient algorithms in terms of time and space complexity.
- Big 'O' notation, is a typical way of describing algorithmic efficiency. The efficiency of an algorithm is expressed as how long it runs in relation to its input.
- Big 'O' notation is used in to describe the performance or complexity of an algorithm.
- We can compare algorithms based on their "order". Order is abbreviated with a capital 'O': for instance 'O' (n^2). This notation is known as Big 'O' notation.
- Big 'O' notation is often used to describe how the size of input data affects an algorithms usage of computational resources.
- We can express the time complexity of a program in terms of the order of magnitude of frequency count using the Big 'O' notation.
- Big 'O' is a characteristic scheme that measures properties of algorithm complexity performance and/or memory requirements.
- In Big 'O' notation the algorithm complexity can be determined by eliminating constant factors in the analysis of the algorithm. Clearly, the complexity function f(n) of an algorithm increases as 'n' increase.

For example:

- Let us find out the algorithm complexity by analyzing the sequential searching algorithm. In the sequential search algorithm we simply try to match the target value against each value in the memory and this process will continue until we find a match or finish scanning the whole elements in the array.

- In the array contains 'n' elements, the maximum possible number of comparisons with the target value will be 'n' i.e. the worst case. That is the target value will be found at the nth position of the array.

    $f(n) = n$

- That is **worst case** is when an algorithm requires a maximum number of iterations or steps to search and find out the target value in the array.

- The **best case** is when the number of steps is as less as possible. If the target value is found in a sequential search array of the first position i.e. we need to compare the target value with only one element from the array, we have found the element by executing only one iteration or by least possible statements.

    $f(n) = 1$

- **Average case** falls between these two extremes case i.e. best and worst case. If the target value is found at the $n/2^{nd}$ position on an average we need to compare the target value with only half of the elements in the array, so

    $f(n) = n/2$

- The complexity function f(n) of an algorithm increases as 'n' increases. The function $f(n) = O(n)$ can be read as "f on n is big O of n" or as "f(n) is of the order n". The total running time or time complexity includes the initializations and several other iterative statements through the loop.

- The generalized form of the theorem is,

    $$f(n) = c_t n^x + c_{t-1} n^{x-1} + c_{t-2} n^{x-2} + \ldots + c_2 n^2 + c_1 n^1 + c_0 n^0$$

    where the constant $c_t > 0$

    Then, $f(n) = O(n^2)$.

Most common computing time of algorithm:

If complexity of algorithms is,

Complexity		Computing time
$O(1)$	=	Constant
$O(n)$	=	Linear
$O(n^2)$	=	Quadratic
$O(n^3)$	=	Cubic
$O(2^n)$	=	Exponential
$O(\log n)$	=	Logarithmic

- Algorithm with exponential running time is not suitable for practical use. $O(\log n)$ is better than $O(2^n)$. For large n, $O(n \log n)$ is better than $O(n^2)$ but not as good as $O(n)$.

- These can be summarized in following Table 1.2.

Table 1.2

n	log n	n log n	n^2	n^3	2^n
1	0	1	1	1	2
2	1	2	4	8	4
4	2	8	16	64	16
8	3	24	64	512	256
16	4	64	256	4096	65536
32	5	160	1024	32768	4294967296
64	6	384	4096	262144	Too large

Limitations of Big 'O' Notation:

1. Big 'O' notation contains no effort to improve the programming methodology.
2. Big 'O' notation does not discuss the way and means to improve the efficiency of the program, but it helps to analyze and calculate the efficiency of the program.
3. Big 'O' notation does not exhibit the potential of the constants.

Algorithm Analysis:

- There are different ways of solving a problem and there are different algorithms which can be designed to solve a problem.
- The goal of analysis of algorithms is to compare algorithms mainly in terms of running time but also in terms of other factors such as memory requirements etc.
- There is a difference between a problem and an algorithm. A problem has a single problem statement that describes it in some general terms. However there are different ways to solve a problem and some of the solutions may be more efficient than the objects.
- Consequently, analysis of algorithms focuses on computation of space and time complexity. Space can be defined in terms of space required to store the instructions and data whereas the time is the computer time an algorithm might require for its execution, which depends on the size of the algorithm and input.
- There are different types of time complexities which can be analyzed for an algorithm:
    1. **Best Case Time Complexity:** It is a measure of the minimum time that the algorithm will require for an input of size 'n'. The running time of many algorithms varies not only for the inputs of different sizes but also for the different inputs of same size. For example in the running time of some sorting algorithms, the sorting will depend on the ordering of the input data. Therefore if an input data of 'n' items is presented in sorted order, the operations performed by the algorithm will take the least time.
    2. **Worst Case Time Complexity:** It is a measure of the maximum time that the algorithm will require for an input of size 'n'. Therefore if various algorithms for

sorting are taken into account and say 'n' input data items are supplied in reverse order for any sorting algorithm, then the algorithm will require n^2 operations to perform the sort which will correspond to the worst case time complexity of the algorithm.

3. **Average Case Time Complexity:** The time that an algorithm will require to execute a typical input data of size 'n' is known as average case time complexity. We can say that the value that is obtained by taking average of the running time of an algorithm for all possible inputs of size 'n' can determine average case time complexity. The computation of exact time taken by the algorithm for its execution is very difficult. Thus the work done by an algorithm for the execution of the input of size 'n' defines the time analysis as function f(n) of the input data items.

1.6 Examples of Algorithms and Flowcharts

1. **Write an algorithm and draw flowchart to input a number to the computer and display the same number on the screen.**

Algorithm:

    Step 1: Start

    Step 2: Enter number A

    Step 3: Display A

    Step 4: Stop

Flowchart:

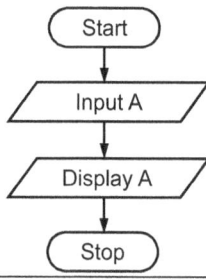

2. **Write an algorithm and flowchart to enter any two numbers and display the sum of two numbers.**

Algorithm:

    Step 1: Start

    Step 2: Input A, B

    Step 3: C = A + B

    Step 4: Output C

    Step 5: Stop

Flowchart:

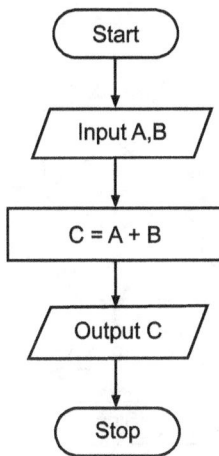

3. **Algorithm and flowchart to convert temperature in celcius to Fahrenheit.**
Algorithm:
- **Step 1:** Start
- **Step 2:** Read C
- **Step 3:** Calculate $F = (C \times 9/5) + 32$
- **Step 4:** Display F
- **Step 5:** Stop

Flowchart:

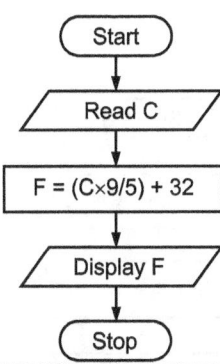

4. **Algorithm and flowchart to input a number to the computer. If number is less than 10, multiply the number by 2, otherwise multiply the number by 3 and display the answer.**
Algorithm:
- **Step 1:** Start
- **Step 2:** Input A
- **Step 3:** If A < 10 then A = A * 2, goto Step 5, otherwise Goto Step 4.
- **Step 4:** A = A * 3
- **Step 5:** Display A
- **Step 6:** Stop.

Flowchart:

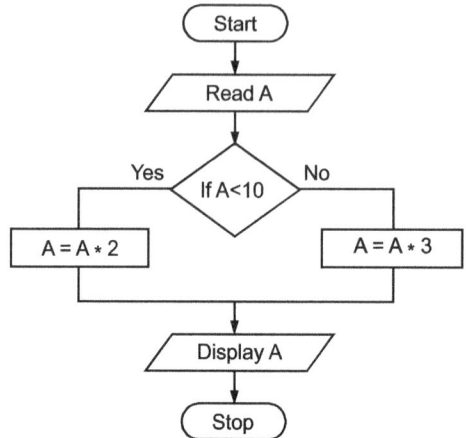

5. **Algorithm and flowchart to input one number and display next 10 numbers in increasing order.**

Algorithm:
   Step 1: Start
   Step 2: Input A
   Step 3: B = A + 10
   Step 4: Output A
   Step 5: A = A + 1
   Step 6: If A ≤ B, Go to Step 4
   Step 7: Stop.

Flowchart:

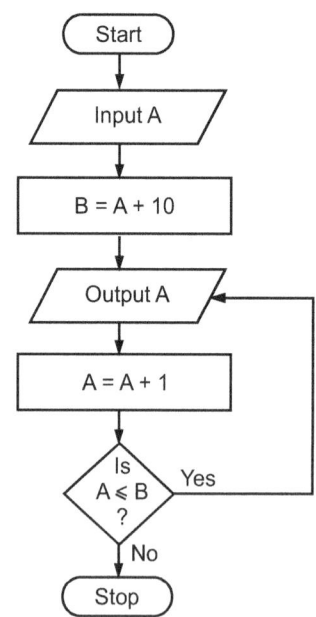

6. Algorithm and flowchart to display 1 through 100 numbers.

Algorithm:
- **Step 1:** Start
- **Step 2:** Let A = 1
- **Step 3:** Display A
- **Step 4:** A = A + 1
- **Step 5:** If A < = 100 Goto Step 3
- **Step 6:** Stop

Flowchart:

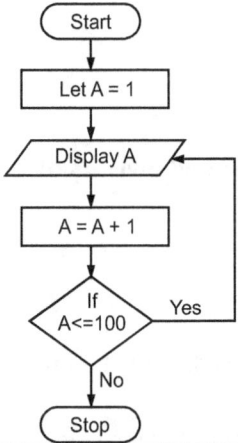

7. Algorithm and flowchart to print all odd numbers between 1 and 100.

Algorithm:

- **Step 1:** Start
- **Step 2:** Let A = 1
- **Step 3:** Display A
- **Step 4:** A = A + 1
- **Step 5:** If A <= 100 then Goto Step 6. Otherwise Goto Step 7.
- **Step 6:** If A MOD2! = 0 then Goto Step 3, Otherwise Goto Step 4.
- **Step 7:** Stop.

Flowchart:

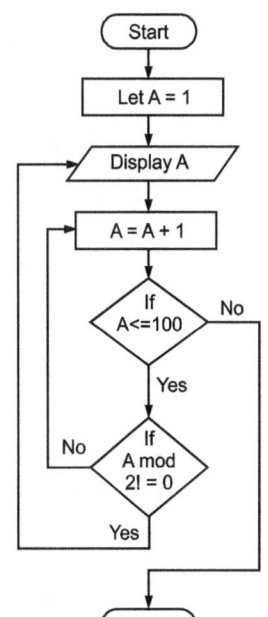

8. Write algorithm and draw flowchart to calculate the area of circle. (Oct. 2014)

Algorithm:

Step 1: Start

Step 2: Input and Read r

Step 3: Area = 3.14 * r * r

Step 4: Print Area

Step 5: Stop.

Flowchart:

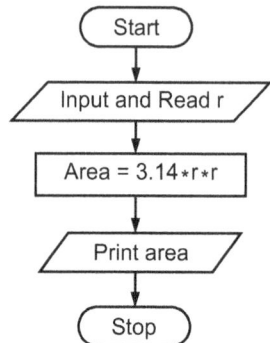

9. Algorithm and flowchart to print all divisors of integer N.

Algorithm:

Step 1: Start
Step 2: Read N
Step 3: Let Ctr = 1
Step 4: If N Mod Ctr = 0 then N is divisible by Ctr, Print Ctr
Step 5: Add 1 to Ctr
Step 6: If Ctr is less than or equal to N then Goto Step 4
Step 7: Stop

Flowchart:

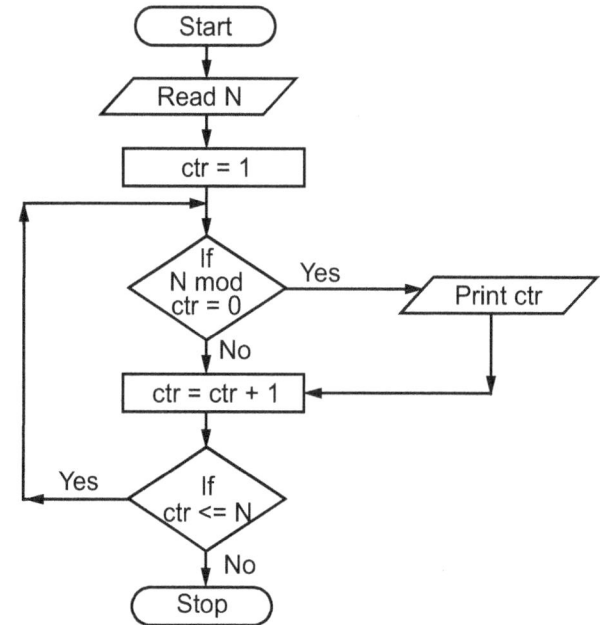

10. Algorithm and flowchart for summation of sequence:
(1 + 1 / 2! + 1 / 3! + 1 / 4! + 1/ 5! + ...)

Algorithm:

Step 1: Start
Step 2: Read the number of terms as N
Step 3: Let Sum = 0 and Counter = 1
Step 4: Let j = 1 and fact = 1
Step 5: Calculate fact = fact * j
Step 6: Add 1 to j
Step 7: If j is less than or equal to Counter then Goto Step 5
Step 8: Calculate Sum = Sum + 1 / fact
Step 9: Add 1 to Counter
Step 10: If Counter is less than or equal to N then Goto Step 4
Step 11: Print the value of Sum
Step 12: Stop.

Flowchart:

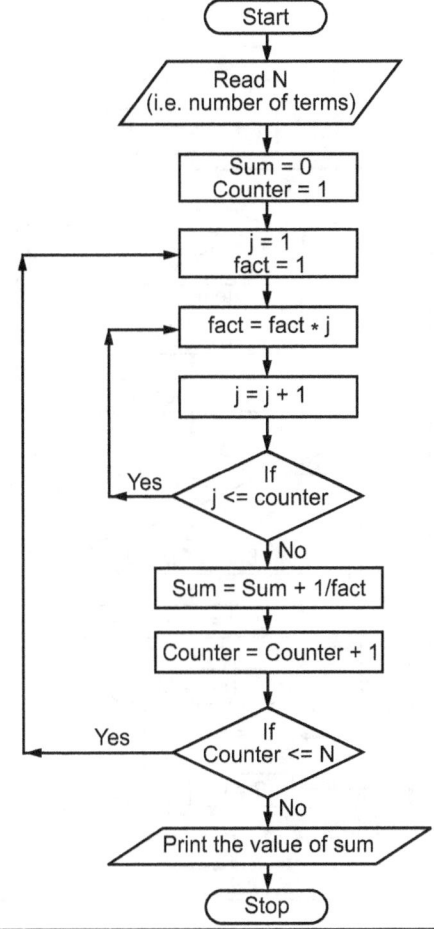

11. Algorithm and flowchart to find LCM and GCD of given 2 numbers.

Algorithm:

Step 1: Start
Step 2: Read A, B
Step 3: Calculate the Product = A * B
Step 4: If A is less than B then swap the two numbers by;
  (a) temp = A
  (b) A = B
  (c) B = temp
Step 5: Calculate R = A Mod B
Step 6: If R = 0 then
  (a) Print GCD = B
  (b) Calculate LCM = Product / B
  (c) Print LCM, Goto Step 8
Step 7: A = B
Step 8: B = R, Goto Step 4
Step 9: Stop.

Flowchart:

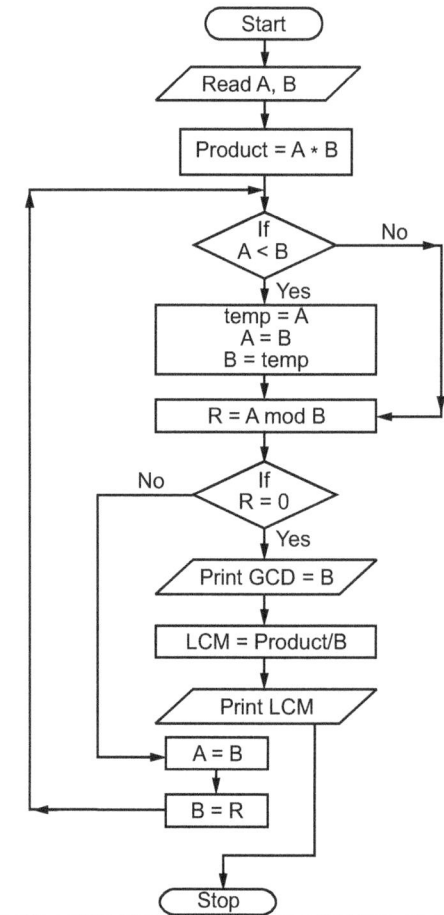

12. Algorithm to print the following Pattern:

```
*
* *
* * *
* * * *
* * *
* *
*
```

Algorithm:

   Step 1: Start

   Step 2: Let Line = 1 be the counter to count the number of lines

   Step 3: Let Cnt = 1 be the counter to count the number of '*' on a particular line

   Step 4: Print '*'

   Step 5: Add 1 to Cnt

   Step 6: if Cnt is less than or equal to Line then Goto Step 4

   Step 7: Print a newline character (bring the cursor to next line)

   Step 8: Add 1 to Line

   Step 9: If line is less than or equal to 4 then Goto Step 3

   Step 10: Let Line = 3

   Step 11: Let Cnt = 1

   Step 12: Print '*'

   Step 13: Add 1 to Cnt

   Step 14: if Cnt is less than or equal to Line then Goto Step 12

   Step 15: Print a newline character (bring the cursor to next line)

   Step 16: Subtract 1 from Line

   Step 17: If line is less than or equal to 1 then Goto Step 11

   Step 18: Stop.

Flowchart:

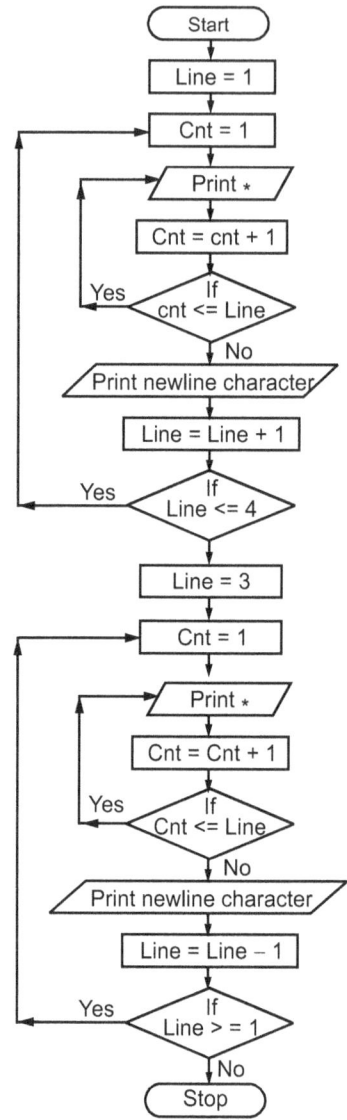

13. Algorithm and flowchart to generate N Fibonacci numbers like 1 1 2 3 5 8 13 21 ...

Algorithm:

Step 1: Start
Step 2: Read N
Step 3: Let First term F1 = 1 & Second term F2 = 1
Step 4: Print F1, F2
Step 5: Let counter = 3

Step 6: Calculate F3 = F1 + F2
Step 7: Print F3
Step 8: Add 1 to counter
Step 9: If counter > N then Goto Step 11
Step 10: F1 = F2, F2 = F3, Goto Step 6
Step 11: Stop.

Flowchart:

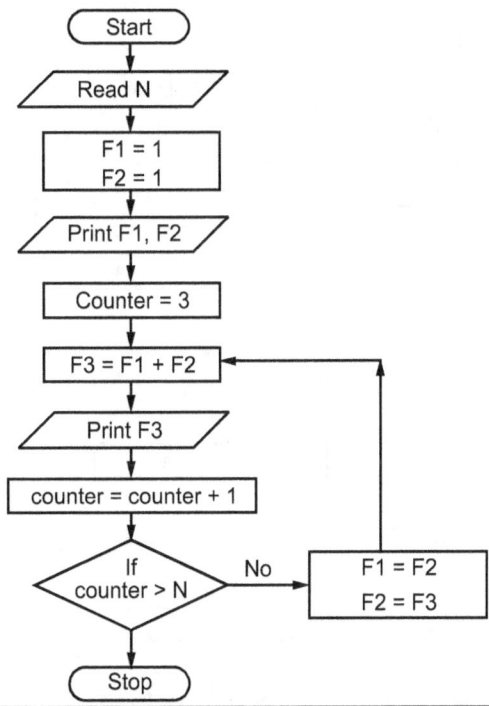

---

14. **Algorithm that reads a set of n single digits and converts them into a single decimal integer. For example, Set of 3 digits { 4, 2, 9 } then it should be converted to 429.**

Algorithm:
   Step 1: Start
   Step 2: Read N
   Step 3: Read corresponding N digits and store it Array digit[ ]
   Step 4: Let Counter = N , Sum = 0 , temp = 1
   Step 5: Sum = Sum + (digit[Counter] * temp)
   Step 6: temp= temp * 10
   Step 7: Counter = Counter – 1
   Step 8: Repeat Steps 5, 6, 7 Until Counter >= 1/If counter >= 1 Goto Step 5.
   Step 9: Print Sum
   Step 10: Stop.

Flowchart:

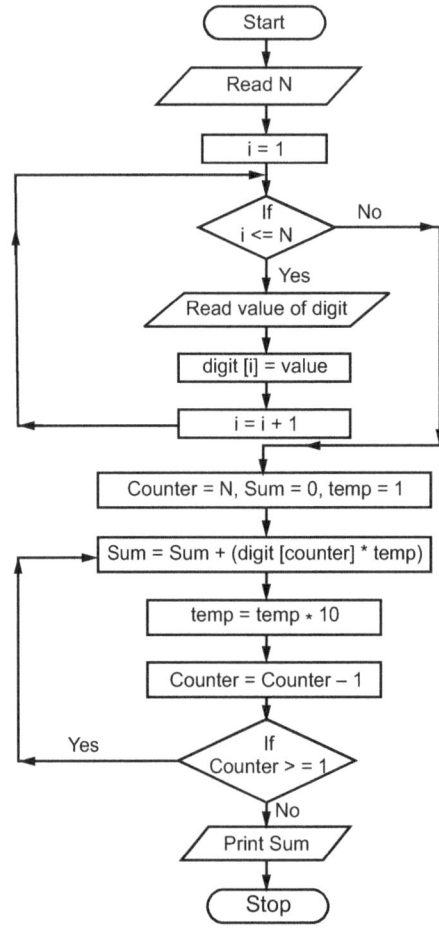

---

15. **Algorithm and flowchart to generate a Sequence in arithmetic progression whose Initial Term and Common Difference is given, Find the Nth term.**

    For example, If Initial term is 2 , Common Difference is 4 Then 6th term is:

    2, 6, 10, 14, 18, 22

    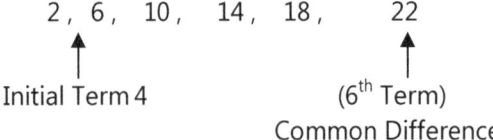

Algorithm:

Step 1: Start
Step 2: Read Initial term as IT
Step 3: Read Common difference as CD
Step 4: Read Last term as N
Step 5: Print IT

Step 6: Let counter = 1
Step 7: Calculate IT = IT + CD
Step 8: Print IT
Step 9: Add 1 to counter
Step 10: If counter is less than N then Goto Step 7.
Step 11: Print newline character
Print IT as N^{th} term
Print N^{th} term separately again as problem statement demands finding N^{th} term too.
Step 12: Stop.

Flowchart:

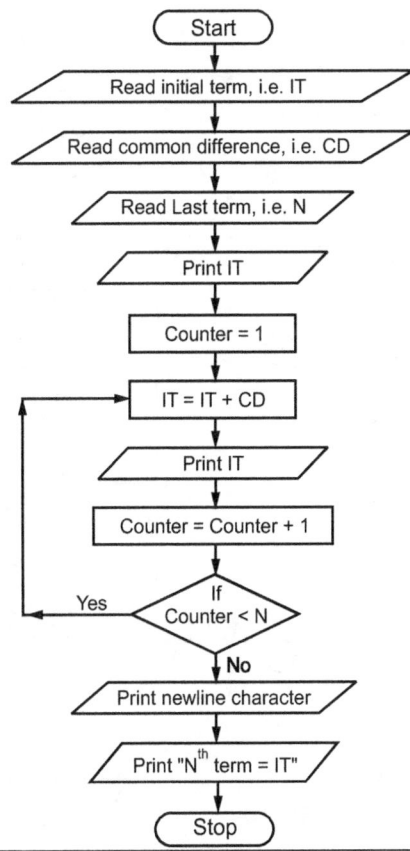

16. Algorithm and flowchart to print a given single digit number into word.

Algorithm:
Step 1: Start
Step 2: Read the number
Step 3: if number = 0 then print 'Zero', Goto Step 13
Step 4: if number = 1 then print 'One', Goto Step 13

Step 5: if number = 2 then print 'Two', Goto Step 13
Step 6: if number = 3 then print 'Three', Goto Step 13
Step 7: if number = 4 then print 'Four', Goto Step 13
Step 8: if number = 5 then print 'Five', Goto Step 13
Step 9: if number = 6 then print 'Six', Goto Step 13
Step 10: if number = 7 then print 'Seven', Goto Step 13
Step 11: if number = 8 then print 'Eight', Goto Step 13
Step 12: if number = 9 then print 'Nine'
Step 13: Stop.

Flowchart:

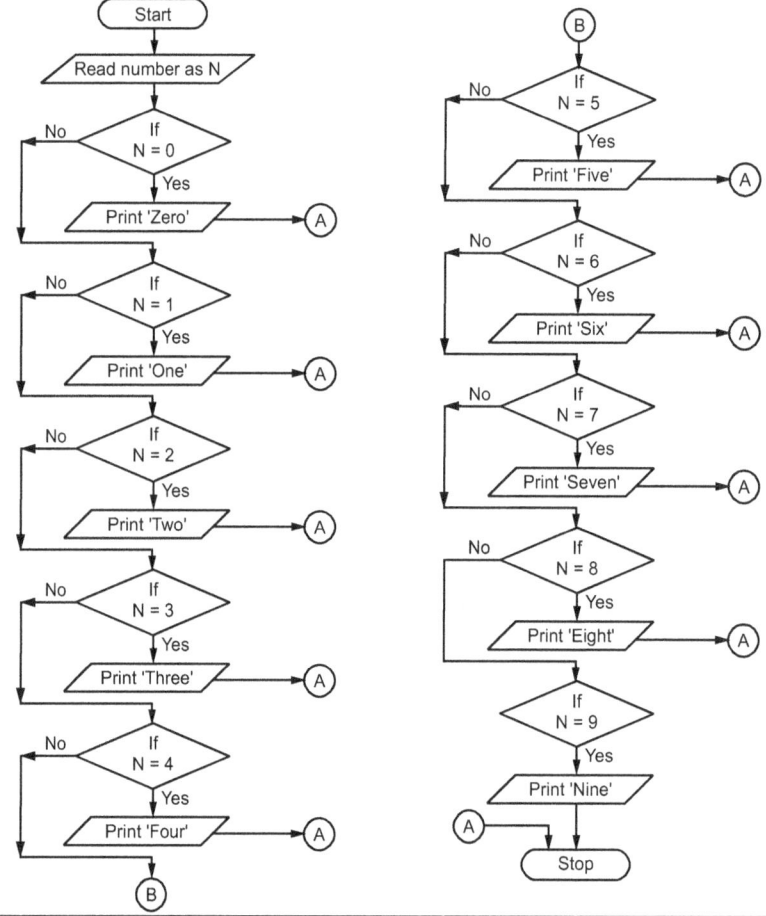

---

17. Write an algorithm and draw flowchart to print all prime numbers in a given range a to b.

Algorithm:
   Step 1: Start
   Step 2: Read a
   Step 3: Read b

Step 4: Let n = a

Step 5: Flag = True and Counter = 2

Step 6: If n MOD Counter = 0 then Flag = False Goto Step 10

Step 7: Add 1 to Counter

Step 8: If Counter < n then Goto Step 6

Step 9: If Flag = True then Print n; Goto Step 11

Step 10: If Flag = False then Goto Step 11.

Step 11: Add 1 to n.

Step 12: If n <= b, then Goto Step 5

Step 13: Stop.

Flowchart:

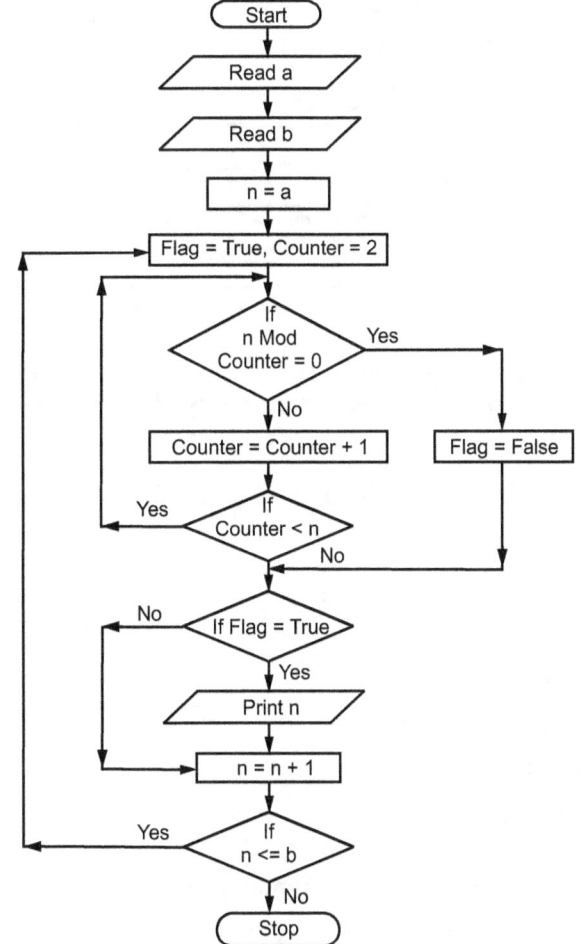

18. Write an algorithm and draw flowchart to check whether an integer m is divisible by another integer n or not.

Algorithm:

Step 1: Start

Step 2: Read m

Step 3: Read n

Step 4: If (m Mod n) = 0 then print 'm is divisible by n' Otherwise print 'm is not divisible by n'

Step 5: Stop.

Flowchart:

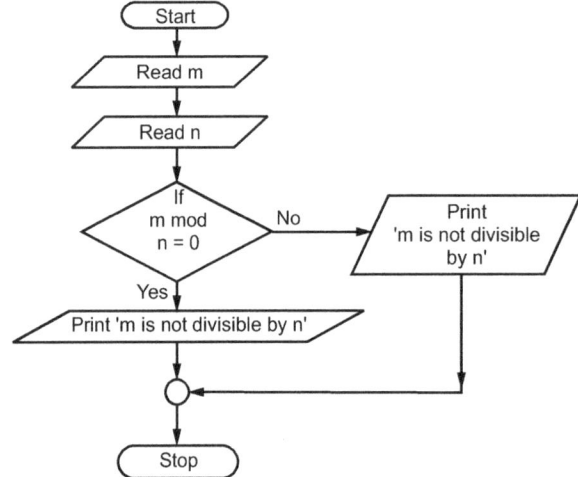

19. Write an algorithm and draw flowchart to check if a given number is a armstrong number. (April 2015)

Algorithm:

Step 1: Start

Step 2: Read N

Step 3: Let Number = N

Step 4: Let Sum = 0

Step 5: Let x = N Mod 10

Step 6: Calculate cube of x as temp

Step 7: Add temp to Sum

Step 8: N = N Div 10

Step 9: If n not equal to 0 then Goto Step 5

Step 10: If Number = Sum then print 'Number is a armstrong number' Otherwise print 'Number is not armstrong number'

Step 11: Stop.

Flowchart:

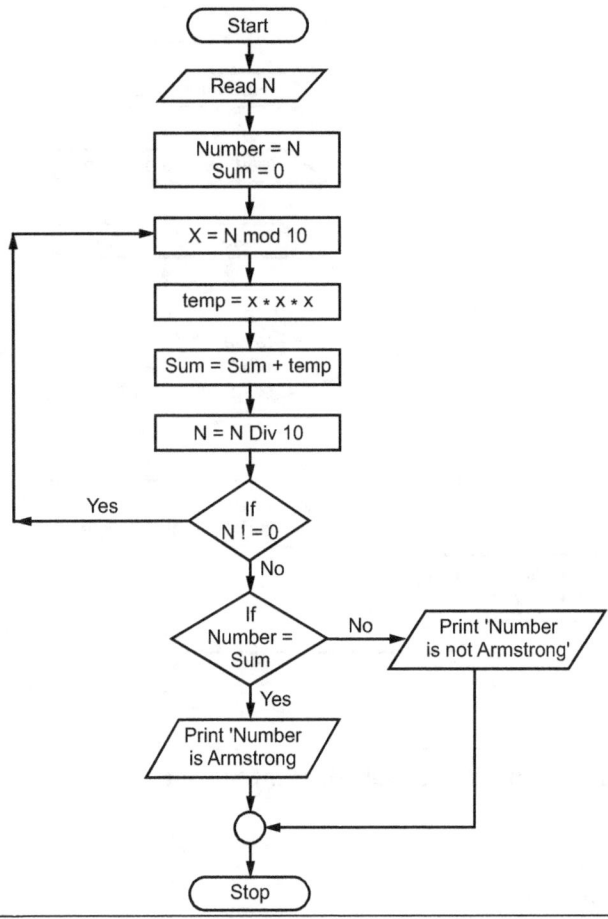

20. Write an algorithm and draw flowchart to check if the given triangle is a right angled triangle or not.

Algorithm:

Step 1: Start

Step 2: Read one side of a triangle as a

Step 3: Read another side of triangle as b

Step 4: Read third side of triangle as c

Step 5: If (a*a = b*b + c*c) OR (b*b = a*a + c*c)

OR (c*c = a*a + b*b) then print 'Triangle is a right angle triangle'
Otherwise print 'Triangle is not a right angle triangle'.

Step 6: Stop.

Flowchart:

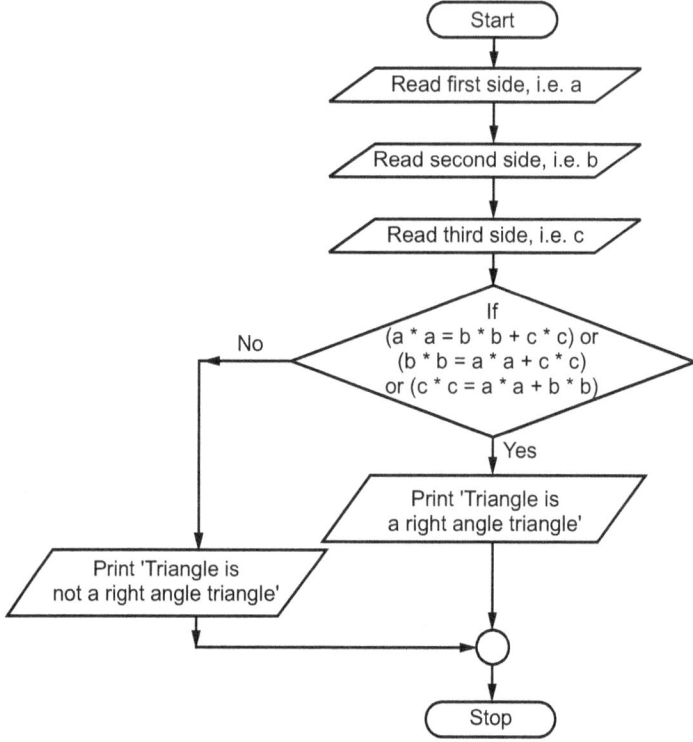

21. Algorithm and flowchart for convert days into months and days.

Algorithm:

Step 1: Start

Step 2: Read days as d

Step 3: Calculate months = d/30

Calculate day = d% 30

Step 4: Write months, days

Step 5: Stop.

Flowchart:

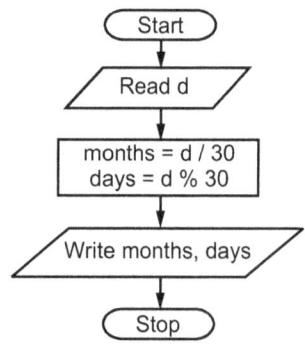

22. Algorithm and flowchart for displaying the grade obtained by a student.

Total Marks	Grade
> 800	A
601-800	B
401-600	C
201-400	D

Algorithm:
   Step 1: Start
   Step 2: Read the marks in four subjects, i.e. sub1, sub2, sub3, sub4
   Step 3: Calculate total=sub1+sub2+sub3+sub4
   Step 4: If total is greater than 800 then Print Grade 'A' Goto Step 8
   Step 5: If total is greater than 600 then Print Grade 'B' Goto Step 8
   Step 6: If total is greater than 400 then Print Grade 'C' Goto Step 8
   Step 7: If total is greater than 200 then Print Grade 'D'
   Step 8: Stop

Flowchart:

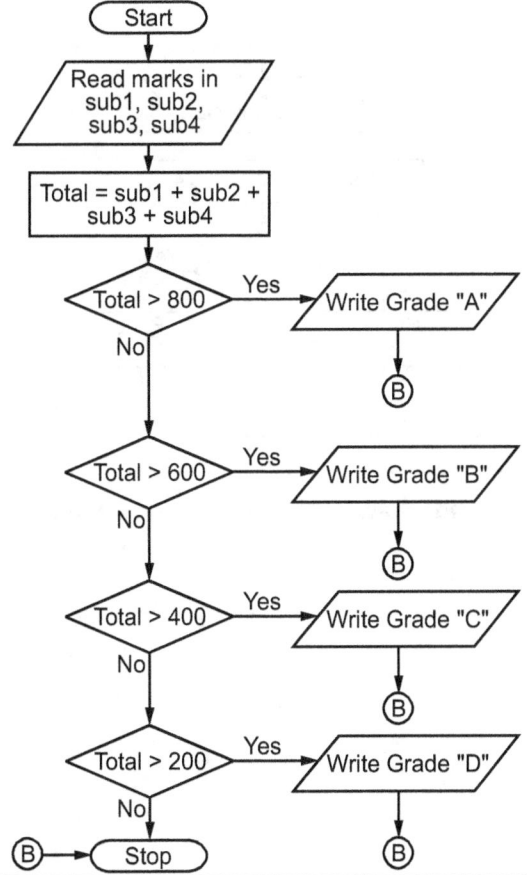

23. Algorithm and flowchart for pass or fail.

Algorithm:

Step 1: Start

Step 2: Input Q_1, Q_2, Q_3, Q_4

Step 3: Grade = $(Q_1 + Q_2 + Q_3 + Q_4)/4$

Step 4: if (Grade < 50) then

        Print "Fail"

  else

        Print "Pass"

Step 5: Stop

Flowchart:

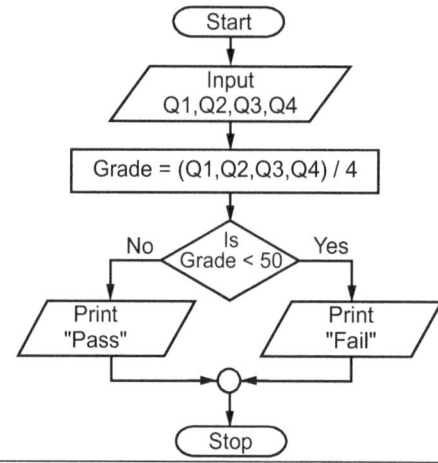

24. Write an algorithm and draw a flowchart to convert the length in feet to centimeter.

Algorithm:

Step 1: Start

Step 2: Input Lft

Step 3: Lcm = Lft × 30

Step 4: Print Lcm

Step 5: Stop.

Flowchart:

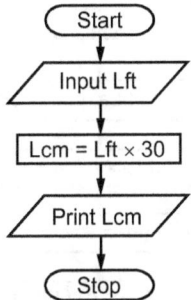

25. Write an algorithm and draw a flowchart that will read the two sides of a rectangle and calculate its area.

Algorithm:
   Step 1: Start
   Step 2: Input W, L
   Step 3: A = L × W
   Step 4: Print A
   Step 5: Stop.

Flowchart:

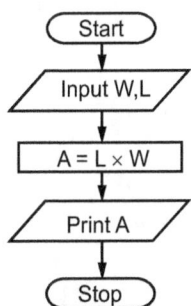

26. Write an algorithm and draw a flowchart that will calculate the roots of a quadratic equation.

$$ax^2 + bx + c = 0$$

Hint: $d = sqrt(b^2 - 4ac)$, and the roots are:
   $x_1 = (-b + d)/2a$ and $x_2 = (-b - d)/2a$

Algorithm:
   Step 1: Start
   Step 2: Input a, b, c
   Step 3: d = sqrt (b × b − 4 × a × c)
   Step 4: x_1 = (−b + d) / (2 × a)
   Step 5: x_2 = (−b − d) / (2 × a)
   Step 6: Print x_1, x_2
   Step 7: Stop.

Flowchart:

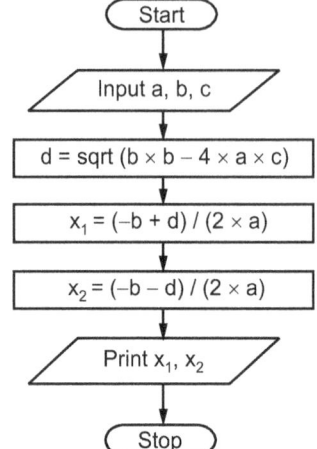

---

27. Write an algorithm and draw flowchart that reads two values, determines the largest value and prints the largest value with an identifying message.

Algorithm:

Step 1: Start

Step 2: Input Value1, Value2

Step 3: if(Value1 > Value2) then

  Max = Value1

 else

  Max = Value2

Step 4: Print "The largest value is", Max

Step 5: Stop.

Flowchart:

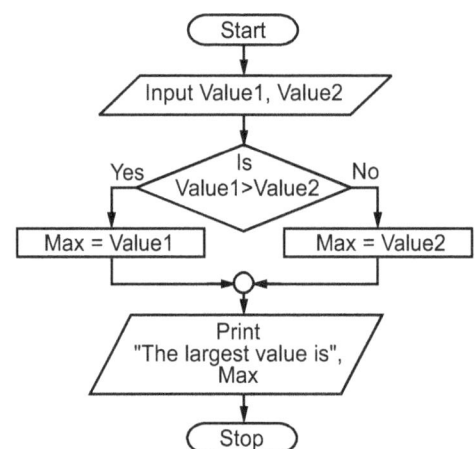

28. Algorithm and flowchart for withdrawal cash from ATM machine.

Algorithm:

Step 1: Start

Step 2: Go to the ATM

Step 3: Insert your card into the machine

Step 4: Press in your code

Step 5: Choose "Withdraw" and enter Amount required

Step 6: Take the cash, slip and card.

Step 7: Stop.

Flowchart:

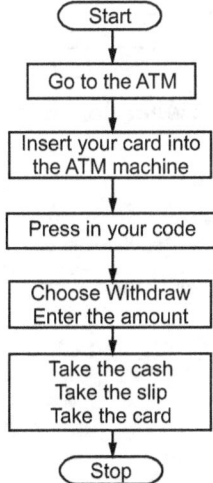

29. Algorithm and flowchart to calculate the interest of a bank deposit. You are to read the amount, years and interest rate from the keyboard and print the interest amount.

Algorithm:

Step 1: Start

Step 2: Read amount

Step 3: Read years

Step 4: Read rate

Step 5: Set interest as amount * Rate * Years / 100

Step 6: Print Interest

Step 7: Stop.

Flowchart:

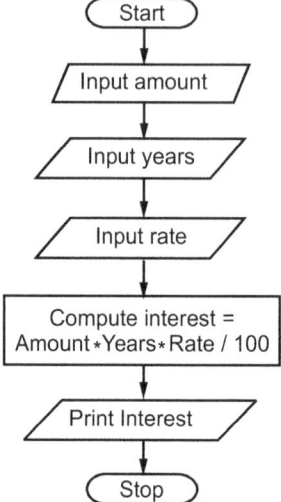

30. Algorithm and Flowchart to print what do when driving to a traffic signal.

Algorithm:

Step 1: Start

Step 2: Read traffic signal

Step 3: If signal is GREEN then set action as GO

   Else

   Set Action as STOP

Step 4: Print Action

Step 5: Stop

Flowchart:

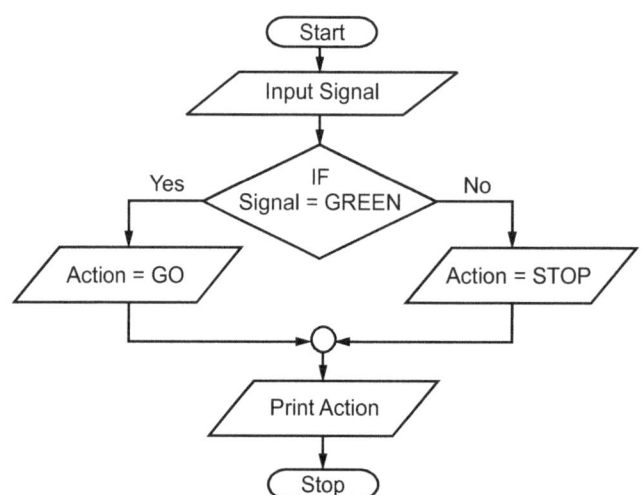

31. Algorithm and flowchart to read a number from the keyboard. Check and output if a given number N is ODD or EVEN.

Algorithm:
- **Step 1:** Start
- **Step 2:** Read N
- **Step 3:** Set remainder as N modulo 2
- **Step 4:** If remainder is equal to 0 then
    Set answer as EVEN
    Else
    Set Answer as ODD
- **Step 5:** Print Answer
- **Step 6:** Stop.

Flowchart:

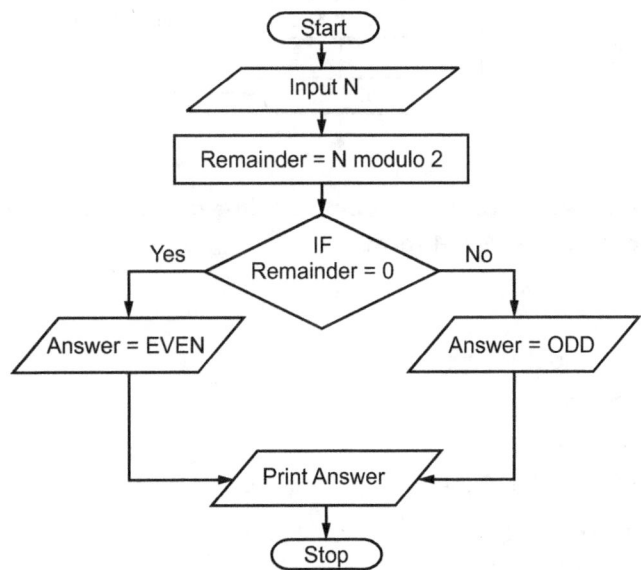

32. Algorithm and flowchart to print title for a person. (Either Mr. or Miss or Mrs.) You are to read the gender (and status if needed).

Algorithm:
- **Step 1:** Start
- **Step 2:** Read Gender
- **Step 3:** If Gender is Male then
    Title is Mr.
    Else
    Read Status
    If Status is Married then
      Title is Mrs.
    Else
      Title is Miss.
- **Step 4:** Print Title
- **Step 5:** Stop

Flowchart:

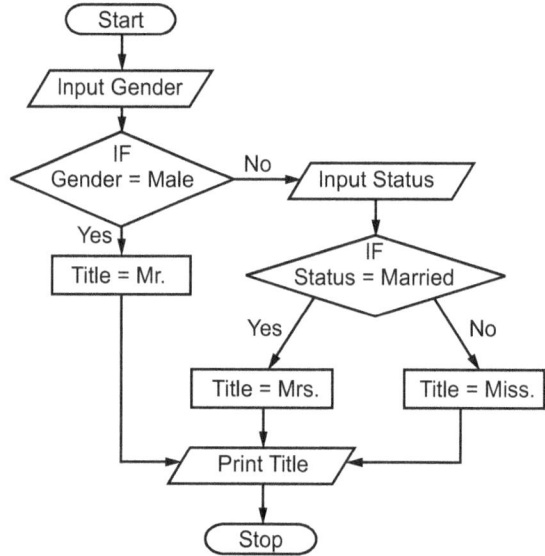

33. Algorithm and flowchart to given computer time is stored in 24 hours format. You are to print the time in AM/PM format.

Algorithm:

Step 1: Start

Step 2: Retrieve computer time

Step 3: Extract hours

Extract minutes

Step 4: If hours is equal to 0 then

    Print 12

Else

    If hours is between 1 and 12 then

        Print hours

    Else

        Print hours - 12

Step 5: Print ':'

Step 6: Print minutes

Step 7: If hours is less than 12 then

    Print AM

    Else

        Print PM

Step 8: Stop

Flowchart:

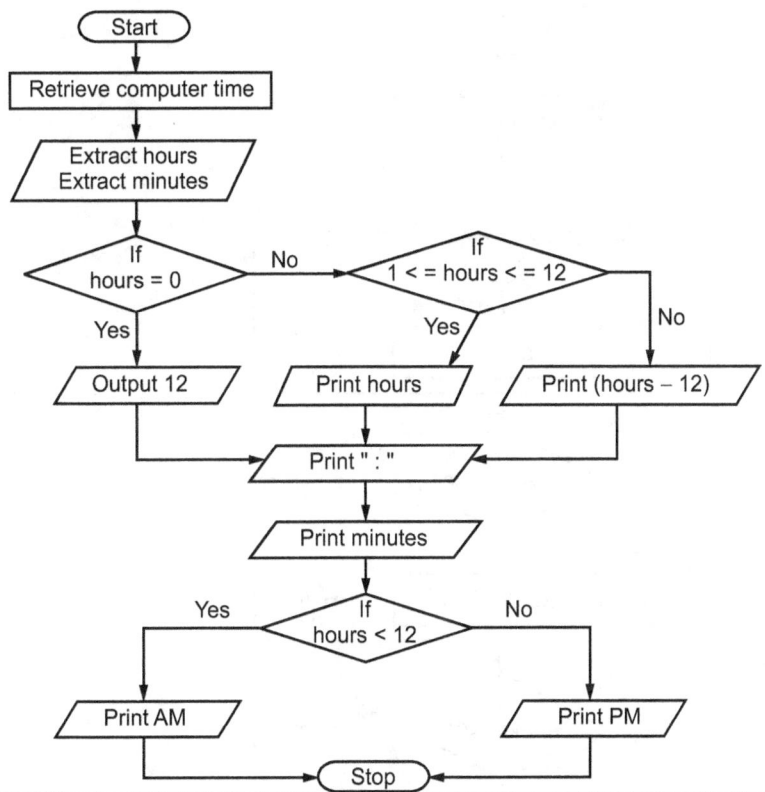

34. A flowchart to read the marks of a student and classify him into different grades. If marks greater than or equal to 90 Grade A, greater than or equal to 80 but less than 90 Grade B, Greater than or equal to 65 but less than 80 Grade C otherwise Grade D.

Algorithm:

   Step 1: Start
   Step 2: Read marks
   Step 3: If marks >= 90
          Declare Grade = "A" Goto Step 4
          Else if marks >= 80 declare
          Grade = "B" Goto Step 4
          Else if marks >= 65 declare
          Grade = "C" Goto step 4
          Else declare Grade = "D"
          Goto Step 4
   Step 4: Write Grade
   Step 5: Stop.

Flowchart:

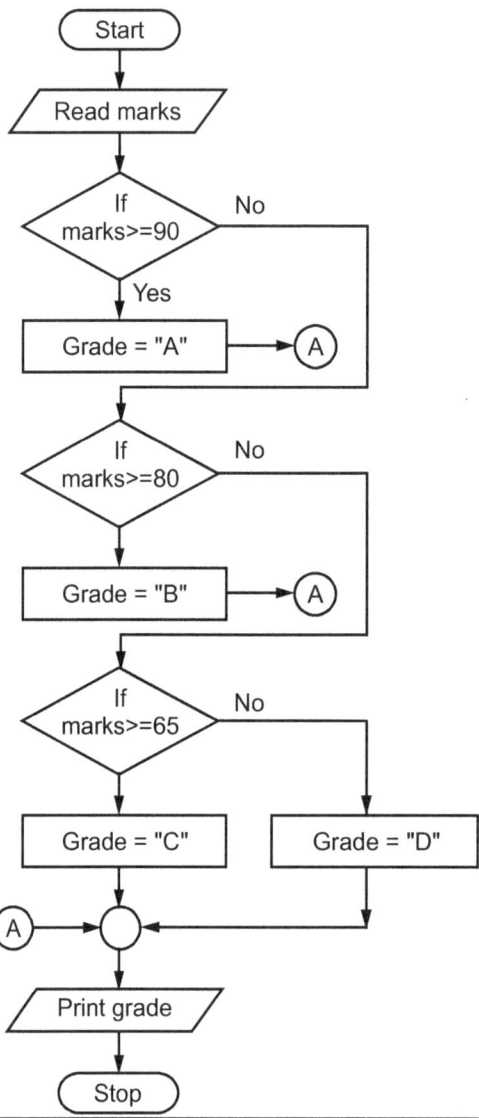

35. Write an algorithm and draw flowchart to find the square of a number.

Algorithm:

    Step 1: Start

    Step 2: Input the Number A

    Step 3: Let Square = A * A

    Step 4: Give the Answer

    Step 5: Stop

Flowchart:

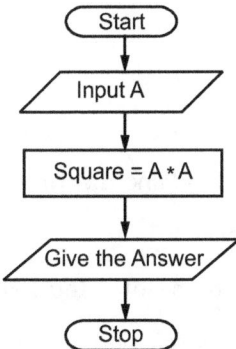

36. Write an algorithm and draw flowchart to make tea.

Algorithm:

Step 1: Start

Step 2: Take water in pan

Step 3: Boil the water

Step 4: Add sugar and tea powder

Step 5: Add milk

Step 6: Boil it (water)

Step 7: Pour it into cup

Step 8: Stop.

Flowchart:

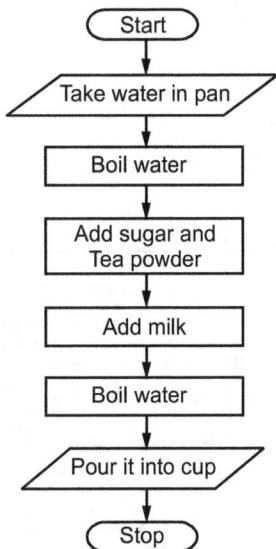

37. Algorithm and flowchart to get two numbers from the user (dividend and divisor) and displaying their quotient.

Algorithm:

Step 1: Start

Step 2: Accept the values of dividend and divisor

Step 3: Print dividend and divisor

Step 4: If divisor is equal to zero then Goto Step 5 Else Goto Step 8

Step 5: Print error message "divisor must be non-zero"

Step 6: Prompt user to enter the divisor

Step 7: Read dividend and divisor and Goto Step 4

Step 8: Calculate quotient=dividend/divisor

Step 9: Print quotient

Step 10: Stop

Flowchart:

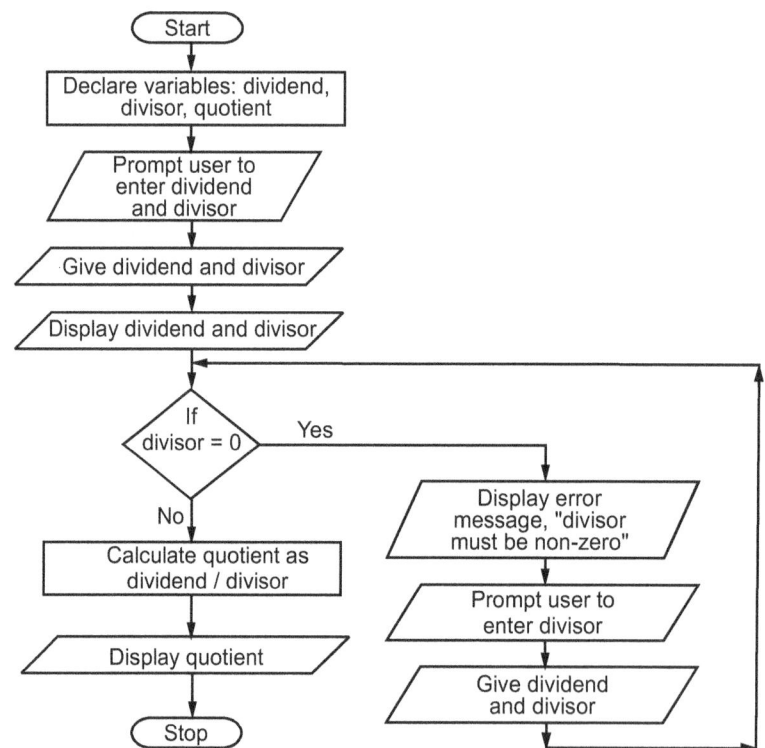

38. Algorithm and flowchart for finding the volume and surface area of a cylinder.

Algorithm:
- **Step 1:** Start
- **Step 2:** Read radius and height as r and h
- **Step 3:** Calculate V = π * r * r * h
- **Step 4:** Calculate A = 2 * π * r * h
- **Step 5:** Print Volume and Area
- **Step 6:** Stop

Flowchart:

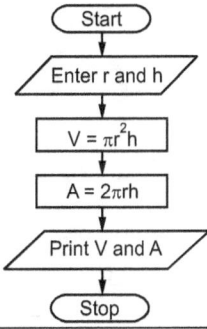

39. Write an algorithm and draw to find the area of a triangle for the given three sides.

Algorithm:
- **Step 1:** Start
- **Step 2:** Declare the floating variables a, b, c, s, area
- **Step 3:** Print the message "enter three sides"
- **Step 4:** Read the values of sides from keyboard
- **Step 5:** Write the logic for s i.e. s = (a + b + c)/2
- **Step 6:** Write the logic for area=root of (s(s − a)(s − b) (s − c))
- **Step 7:** Print the area.
- **Step 8:** Stop

Flowchart:

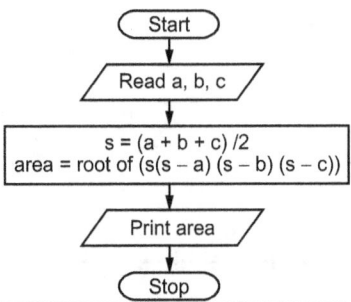

40. Algorithm and flowchart for Victor Construction Company plans to give a 5% year-end bonus to each of its employees earning ₹ 5,000 or more per year and a fixed ₹ 250 bonus to the other employees. The flowchart and algorithm for calculation of bonus for an employee is as shown in below.

Algorithm:
- **Step 1:** Start
- **Step 2:** Read salary of an employee
- **Step 3:** If salary is greater than or equal to 5,000 Then

Calculate Bonus = 0.05 * Salary Goto Step 4
Else Calculate Bonus = 250
Step 4: Write Bonus of Employee
Step 5: Stop
Flowchart:

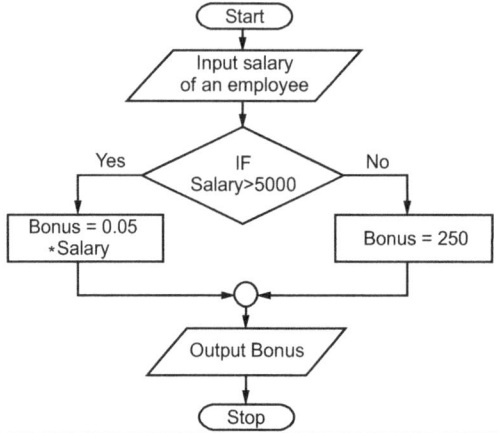

41. Algorithm and flowchart to find the Fibonacci series till term <= 1000.

Step 1: Start
Step 2: Let fterm=0, sterm=1
Step 3: If sterm is less than or equal to 1000 then perform steps 4, 5, 6 and 7
Step 4: Print sterm
Step 5: Set temp=sterm
Step 6: Set sterm=sterm+fterm
Step 7: Set fterm=temp Goto Step 3
Step 8: Stop

Flowchart:

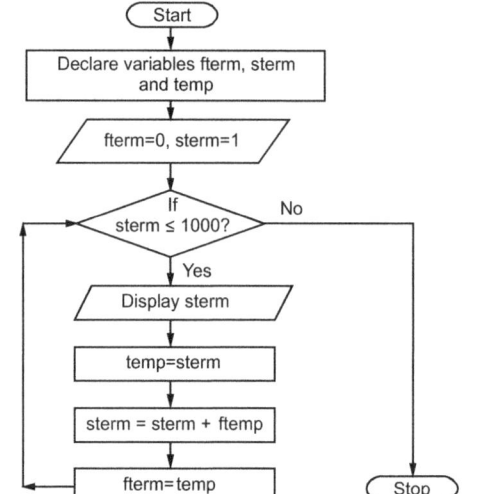

42. Algorithm and flowchart for ATM machine.
Algorithm:
    Step 1: Start
    Step 2: Set attempt=1
    Step 3: Insert ATM card into the slot
    Step 4: If attempts used are less than or equal to 3 then perform Steps 5 to 13 Else Goto Step 15
    Step 5: Choose language reference
    Step 6: Enter PIN number
    Step 7: If data entered is OK then perform Steps 8 to 13
    Else

Attempt=attempt+1 Goto Step 3
Step 8: Select type of transaction, i.e. balance inquiry, withdrawal
Step 9: If type of transaction is balance inquiry then Print the balance Goto step 14
Else Goto Step 10
Step 10: Read the amount for withdrawl
Step 11: If the amount is less than the account balance, then perform steps 12 to 13
Else Print Error Message "Enter Proper Amount" Goto Step 14
Step 12: Collect the cash at the cash dispenser
Step 13: Print the receipt
Step 14: Stop

Flowchart:

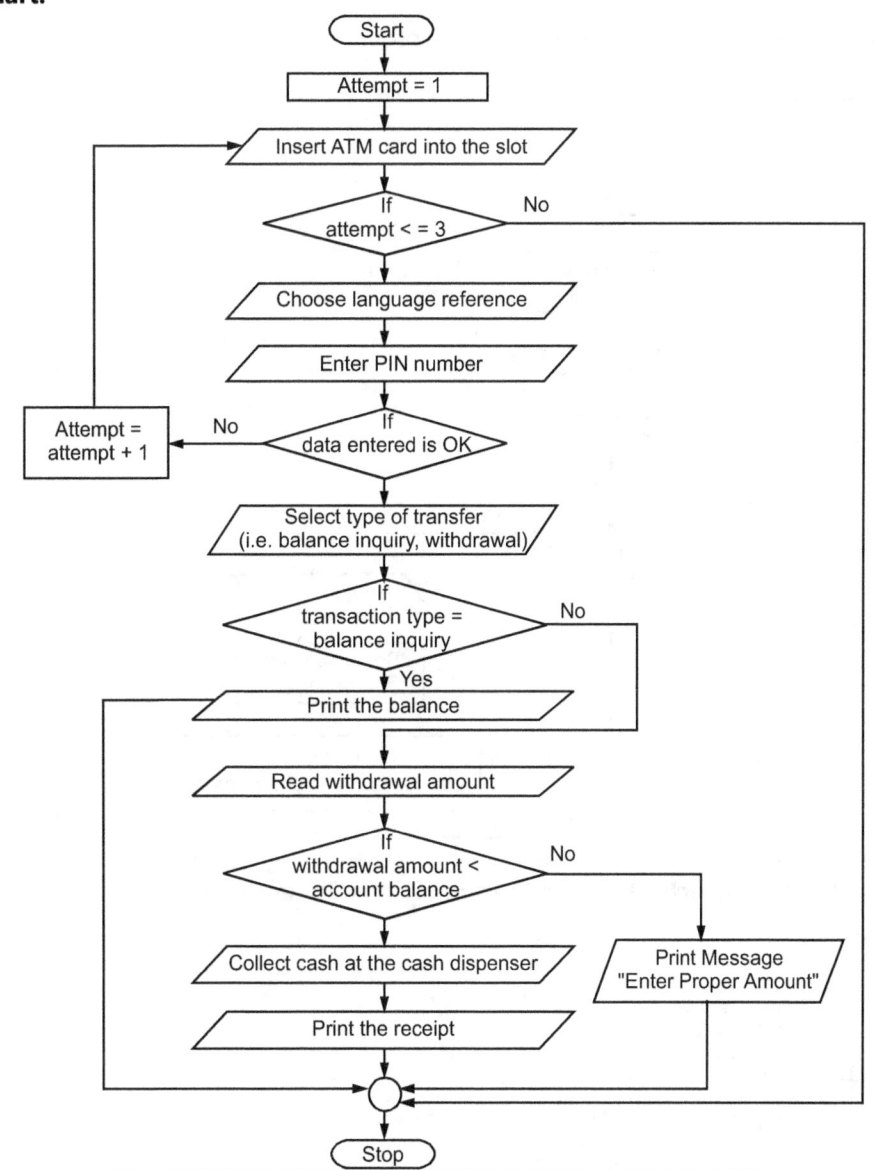

43. Algorithm and flowchart for order processing.

Algorithm:

Step 1: Start

Step 2: Receive order via e-mail

Step 3: Copy and paste e-mail data into database

Step 4: If shipping of order required then perform Steps 5 to 7

Step 5: Print invoice

Step 6: Send e-mail to confirm shipping of order

Step 7: Assemble the package and ship the order

Step 8: Stop

Flowchart:

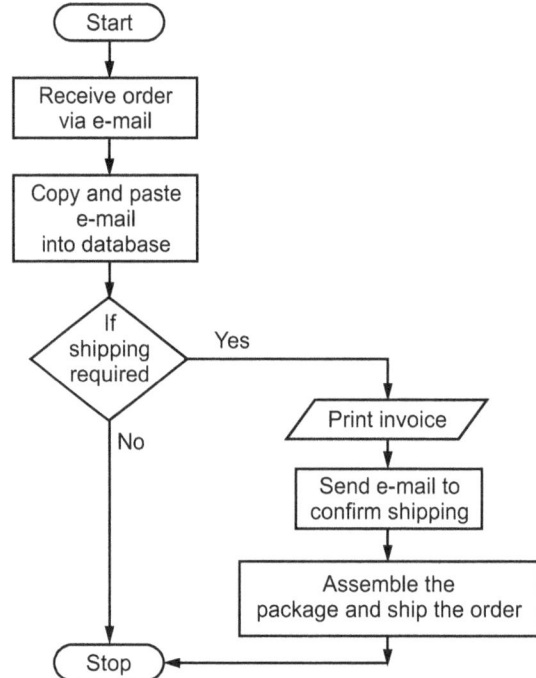

44. Algorithm and flowchart to find the sum of first 50 natural numbers.

Algorithm:

Step 1: Start

Step 2: Let Sum = 0

Step 3: N = 0

Step 4: Increment value of N by 1, i.e. N = N + 1

Step 5: Add N in sum i.e. Sum = Sum + N

Step 6: If N is equal to 50 then Print Sum Goto Step 7
   Else
   Goto Step 4
Step 7: Stop

Flowchart:

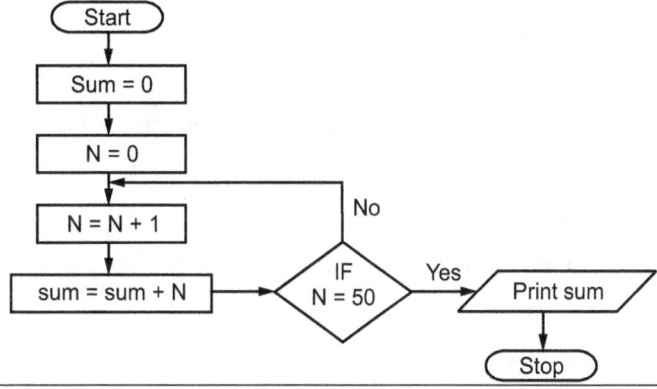

45. Algorithm and flowchart to print the absolute value of a number entered by user.

Algorithm:
   Step 1: Start
   Step 2: Read N
   Step 3: If N is less than zero then Abs=N*(-1) Goto Step 5
   Step 4: Abs=N
   Step 5: Print Abs
   Step 6: Stop

Flowchart:

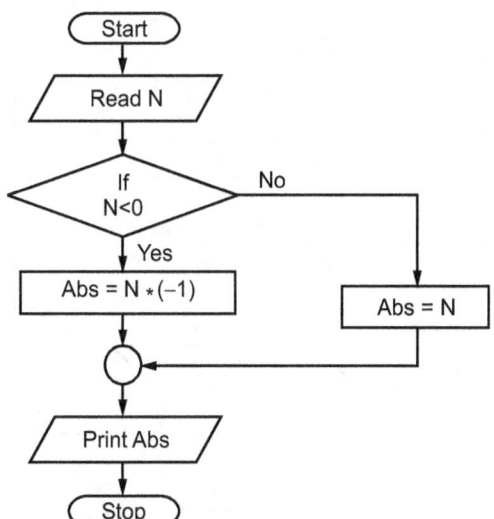

46. Algorithm and flowchart for buying the item whose rate is read from the user and displaying the quantity bought. You can buy items of cost equal to amount.

Algorithm:

Start 1: Start

Start 2: Read amount

Start 3: Read the rate of item

Start 4: Set qty=0

Start 5: If rate is less than or equal to Amount then Goto step 6 Else Goto Step 10

Start 6: Increase qty by 1, i.e. qty=qty+1

Start 7: Calculate Price=qty*rate

Start 8: If Amount – Price is greater than or equal to rate then Goto Step 6

Start 9: Print qty

Start 10: Stop.

Flowchart:

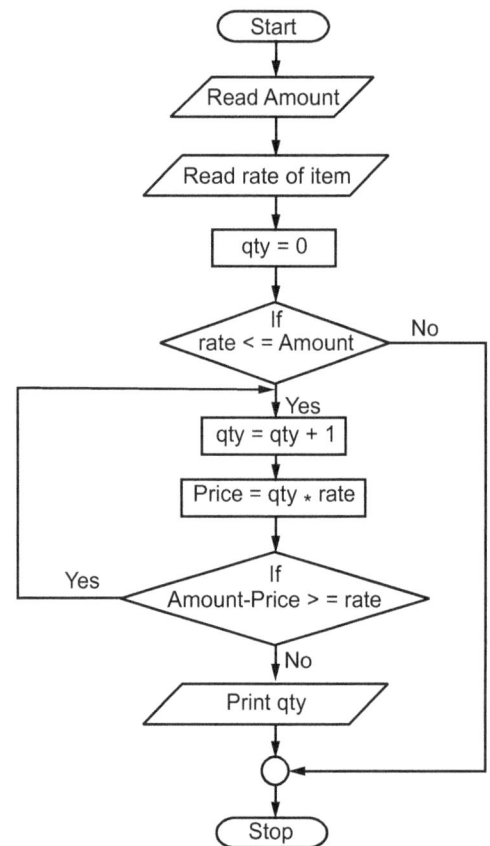

Questions

1. What is problem?
2. Define the following terms:
   (i) Problem
   (ii) Problem solving.
3. With neat diagram explain problem solving steps.
4. Describe problem solving technique in detail.
5. Write short notes on:
   (i) Trial and error,
   (ii) Brainstorming, and
   (iii) Divide and conquer
6. List out different steps of problem solving.
7. Define flowchart. State its advantages and disadvantages.
8. Give uses of algorithms in detail.
10. Give principles of flowcharting in brief.
11. Explain flowchart symbols diagrammatically.
12. Draw a flowchart to display working of ATM.
13. Compare flowchart and algorithm.
14. Define the following terms:
    (i) Flowchart
    (ii) Algorithm
    (iii) Time complexity
15. What is algorithm? State its characteristics.
16. What is complexity?
17. Write short note on: Algorithm analysis.
18. Describe time complexity in detail.
19. What is space complexity?
20. Draw flowchart for library system with algorithm.
21. State advantages and disadvantages of algorithm.
22. Compare time and space complexities.

University Questions and Answers

October 2014

1. What is an algorithm? [2M]
Ans. Please refer to Section 1.3.
2. What is Big-O notation? [2M]
Ans. Please refer to Section 1.5.4.
3. Define time complexity. [2M]
Ans. Please refer to Section 1.5.2.
4. Explain space complexity with example. [4M]
Ans. Please refer to Section 1.5.3.
5. Explain any one problem solving technique. [4M]
Ans. Please refer to Section 1.1.2.3.
6. Explain program development life cycle. [4M]
Ans. Please refer to Section 1.2.
7. Explain different symbols of flowcharts. [4M]
Ans. Please refer to Section 1.4.2.
8. Explain characteristics of algorithm. [4M]
Ans. Please refer to Section 1.3.2.
9. Write an algorithm to calculate area of circle for given radius. [4M]
Ans. Please refer to Section 1.6 Example No. 8.

April 2015

1. What is an algorithm? [2 M]
Ans. Please refer to Section 1.3.
2. Define time complexity. [2 M]
Ans. Please refer to Section 1.5.2.
3. What is flowchart? [2 M]
Ans. Please refer to Section 1.4.
4. Write advantages and disadvantages of algorithms. [4 M]
Ans. Please refer to Section 1.3.4.
5. Explain different approaches for designing an Algorithm. [4 M]
Ans. Please refer to Section 1.3.
6. Explain program developing life cycle. [4 M]
Ans. Please refer to Section 1.2.
7. Explain symbols of flowcharts. [4 M]
Ans. Please refer to Section 1.4.2.
8. Draw a flowchart to check given number is Armstrong or not. [4 M]
Ans. Please refer to Section 1.6 Example No. 19.

✱✱✱

Chapter 2...

Simple Arithmetic Problems

Contents ...

- 2.1 Introduction
    - 2.1.1 Addition of Integers
    - 2.1.2 Multiplication of Integers
    - 2.1.3 Determining if a Number is +ve/−ve
    - 2.1.4 Determining if a Number is Even/Odd
    - 2.1.5 Maximum of Two Distinct Numbers
    - 2.1.6 Maximum of Three Distinct Numbers
    - 2.1.7 Sum of First N Natural Numbers
    - 2.1.8 Sum of First N Given Numbers
    - 2.1.9 Reversing the Digits
    - 2.1.10 Generation of Table for a Given Number N
    - 2.1.11 Computation of Power
    - 2.1.12 ^nC_r (Combinations)
    - 2.1.13 Pascal Triangle
    - 2.1.14 Sine Series
    - 2.1.15 Cosine Series
    - 2.1.16 Prime Numbers
    - 2.1.17 Factors of a Number
    - 2.1.18 Perfect Number
    - 2.1.19 GCD of Two Numbers
    - 2.1.20 Factorial of a Number
    - 2.1.21 Other Algorithms and Flowcharts
- Questions
- University Questions and Answers

2.1 Introduction

- To write effective computer program, one must plan the logic of the program. This logic is written into steps.
- It is necessary that every instruction is written in the proper sequence. The programmer has to write each and every step for solving a given problem. This process is algorithm writing.
- Algorithms can also be expressed in the form of flowcharts.
- Flowchart is a pictorial representation of an algorithm. It has special boxes of different shapes for specific purpose i.e. to denote different types of instructions.
- Simple algorithm and flowchart to Read a number to the computer and display on the screen.

   Algorithm:

   Step 1: Start

   Step 2: Read number N

   Step 3: Display number N

   Step 4: Stop

   Flowchart:

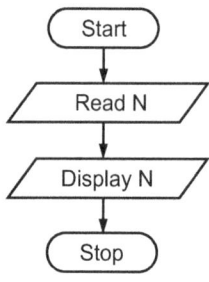

Description:
- The algorithm and flowchart above, illustrate the steps for solving the problem of program for read number to the computer and display on screen.
- Both the algorithm and flowchart should always have a start step at the beginning of the algorithm.
- In this example computer read the number from user and display on screen.

   For example,

   Step 1: Start

   Step 2: Read N = 12

   Step 3: Display the value of N = 12

   Step 4: Stop

2.1.1 Addition of Integers

- Following algorithm and flowchart illustrate the steps for solving the problem of program for addition of two integers. Suppose we take two positive integers say x and y then one can add the both positive integers as x+y and the result is stored in third integer z.

    Algorithm:

    Step 1: Start

    Step 2: Read numbers x and y

    Step 3: z = x + y.

    Step 4: Display z

    Step 5: Stop

    Flowchart:

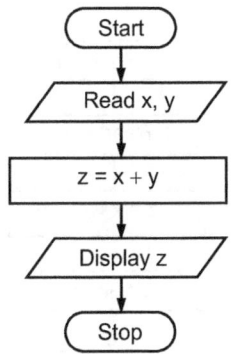

Description:

- Both the algorithm and flowchart should always have a start step at the beginning.

    In step 2 computer read number x and y. In Step 3 calculate the value of z by using formula z = x + y.

- In Step 4 it display the value of z.

    For example,

    Step 1: Start

    Step 2: x = 16, y = 12

    Step 3: z = x + y

    = 16 + 12

    = 28

    Step 4: Display the value of z is 28.

    Step 5: Stop.

2.1.2 Multiplication of Integers (Oct. 2014)

- Following algorithm and flowchart illustrate the steps for solving the problem of program for multiplication of two integers.
- Suppose we take two positive integers say x and y then one can multiply both the positive integers as x * y and the result is stored in third integer z.

Algorithm:

    Step 1: Start

    Step 2: Read numbers x and y

    Step 3: z = x * y.

    Step 4: Display z

    Step 5: Stop

Flowchart:

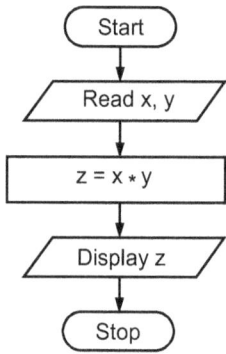

Description:

- Above algorithm and flowchart illustrate the steps for solving the problem of program for multiplication of two numbers.
- Both the algorithm and flowchart should always have a start step at the beginning.
  In Step 2: Computer read number x and y.
  In Step 3: Computer calculate the value of z.
  In Step 4: It display the value of z.
  For example,
  Step 1: Start
  Step 2: x = 80, y = 2
  Step 3: z = x * y
            = 80 * 2
            = 160
  Step 4: Display the value of z = 160.
  Step 5: Stop

2.1.3 Determining if a Number is +ve/−ve

- Negative numbers are on the left side of zero and positive numbers are on the right side of zero, (See Fig. 2.1).

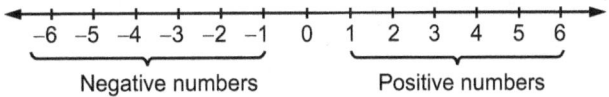

Fig. 2.1

Algorithm:

Step 1: Start

Step 2: Read number as N

Step 3: If N > 0

    Print 'N' is a positive number

    Else

    Print 'N' is a negative number

Step 4: Stop

Flowchart:

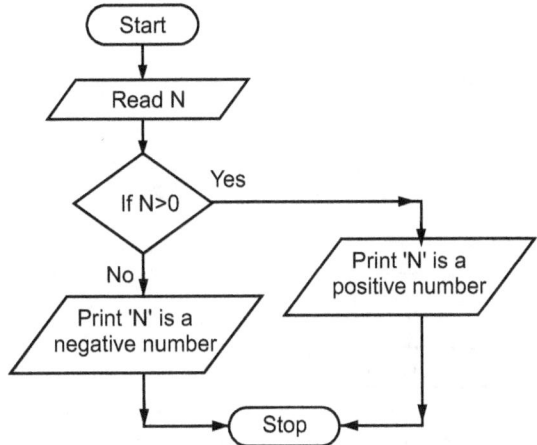

Description:

- Above algorithm and flowchart illustrate the steps for solving the problem of program for determining its number is +ve or −ve.
- Both the algorithm and flowchart should always have a start step at the beginning.

In Step 2: Computer read number as N.

In Step 3: The number is greater than 0. It displays number is positive.

In Step 4: The number is less than 0. It displays number is negative.

For example,

    Step 1: Start

    Step 2: N = 12

    Step 3: N > 0. It display number is positive

    Step 4: Stop

2.1.4 Determining if a Number is Even/Odd

- The numbers can be divided evenly into groups of two is called as Even numbers. The number four can be divided into two groups of two.
- The numbers can not be divided evenly into groups of two is called as Odd numbers. The number five can be divided into two groups of two and one group of one.
- Following Fig. 2.2 shows even and odd numbers.

1	2	3	4	5	6	7	8	9	10	11	12
Odd	Even	Odd	Even	Odd	Even	Odd	Even	Odd	Even	Odd	Even

Fig. 2.2

Algorithm:

    Step 1: Start

    Step 2: Read number as N

    Step 3: If (N mod 2) = 0, then

        Display "N is even"

        Otherwise display "N is odd".

    Step 4: Stop

Flowchart:

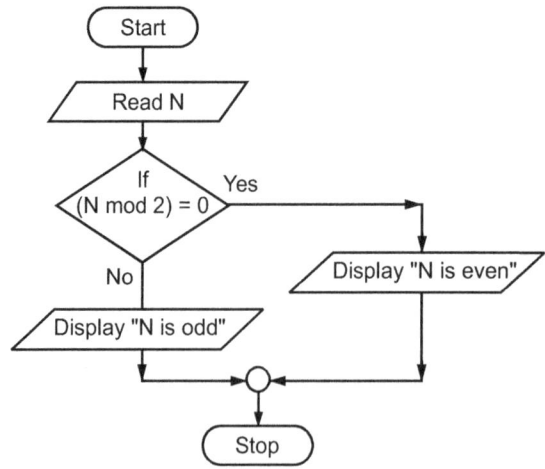

Description:
- Above algorithm and flowchart illustrate the steps for solving the problem of program for determining if a number is even or odd.
- Both the algorithm and flowchart should always have a start step at the beginning.

    In Step 2:   Read number N

    In Step 3:   Calculate

                       N mod 2 = (N%2) = 0, then display N is even.

                       Otherwise display N is odd.

For example,

    Step 2: N = 12

    Step 3: (N%2) = 0

                Display N is even

2.1.5 Maximum of Two Distinct Numbers

- Following algorithm and flowchart illustrate the steps for solving the problem of maximum of two numbers.
- Suppose we take two integers a and b with some value then comparing the value of a and b using the < (less than) or > (greater than) relational operators.

Algorithm:

    Step 1: Start

    Step 2: Read number a and b

    Step 3: If a > b then Display "a is greater"

                 Otherwise Display "b is greater".

    Step 4: Stop

Flowchart:

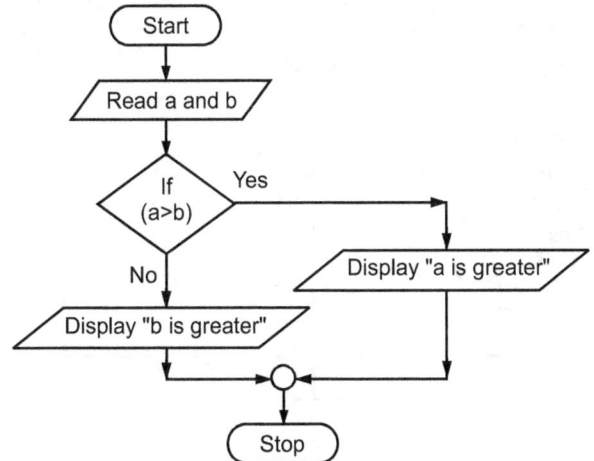

Description:
- Both the algorithm and flowchart above should always have a start step at the beginning.

  Step 2: Read the number 'a' and 'b'

  Step 3: If a>b, then display "a" is greater otherwise "b" is greater.

  Step 4: Stop.

For example,

  Step 2: a = 20, b = 10

  Step 3: (20 > 10)

  This line prints "a" is greater.

  Step 4: Stop.

2.1.6 Maximum of Three Distinct Numbers (April 2015)

- Suppose we take three integers A, B and C with some value then comparing the value of A, B and C using the < (less than) or > (greater than) relational operators.

  Algorithm:

  Step 1: Start

  Step 2: Read A, B, C

  Step 3: Assign max = A

  Step 4: If A > B and A > C then max = A

  Step 5: If B > A and B > C then max = B

  Step 6: If C > A and C > B then max = C

  Step 7: Stop

  Flowchart:

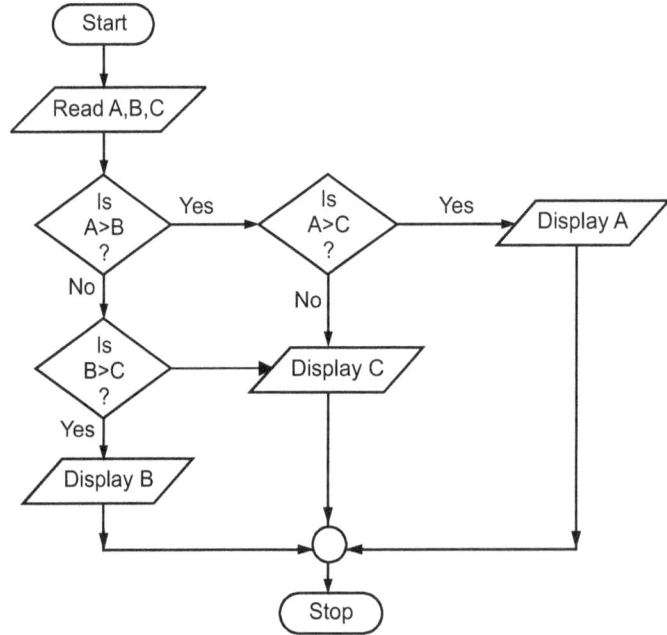

Description:
- Above algorithm and flowchart illustrate the steps for solving the problem of program for determining maximum number among three given numbers.
- Both algorithm and flowchart should always have start step at the beginning.

In Step 2: Computer read A, B and C As A = 25, B = 30, C = 35
In Step 3: Assign max = A
In Step 4: If 'A' is greater than 'B' and 'A' is greater than 'C' then display B is greater. A ≯ B, and A ≯ C.
In Step 5: If 'B' is greater than A and B is greater than 'C' then display B is greater. B > A but B ≯ C.
In Step 6: If 'C' is greater than A and C is greater than B then display 'C' is greater. C > A and C > B. It displays 'C' is greater.

2.1.7 Sum of First N Natural Numbers (Oct. 2014)

- Let's look at this problem for n = 1, 2, 3, 4, 5 and 6 and calculate the sum.

    1 = 1
    1 + 2 = 3
    1 + 2 + 3 = 6
    1 + 2 + 3 + 4 = 10
    1 + 2 + 3 + 4 + 5 = 15
    1 + 2 + 3 + 4 + 5 + 6 = 21

Algorithm:

Step 1: Start
Step 2: Initialize Sum = 0 and X = 0
Step 3: Read N
Step 4: If X<=N
   Sum = Sum + X
   X = X + 1
Step 5: Else Display Sum
Step 6: Stop

Flowchart:

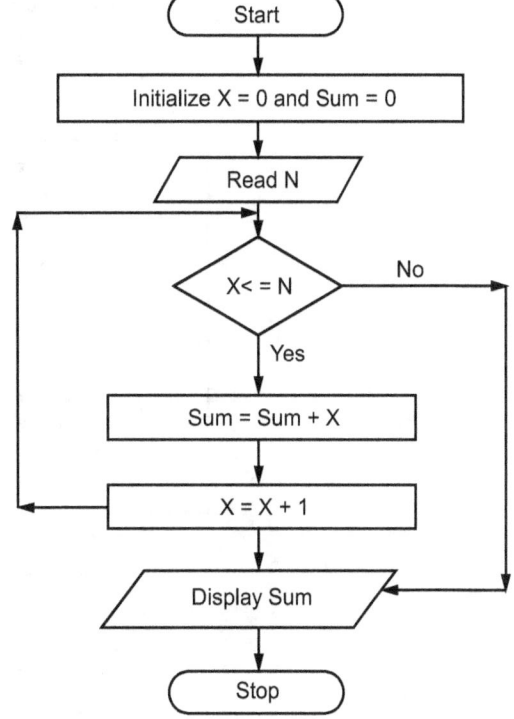

2.1.8 Sum of First N Given Numbers (April 2015)

- Here, the numbers are input by users. If user enters 3, 4, 5 and 6 then sum will be as,
    0 + 3 = 3
    3 + 4 = 7
    7 + 5 = 12
    12 + 6 = 18

Algorithm:
  Step 1: Start
  Step 2: Input and Read N
  Step 3: Put Y = 0 and I = 1
  Step 4: If I<=N
  Step 5: Read number (say Z)
  Step 6: Y = Y + Z
  Step 7: I = I + 1 Goto Step 4
  Step 8: Print Y
  Step 9: Stop

Flowchart:

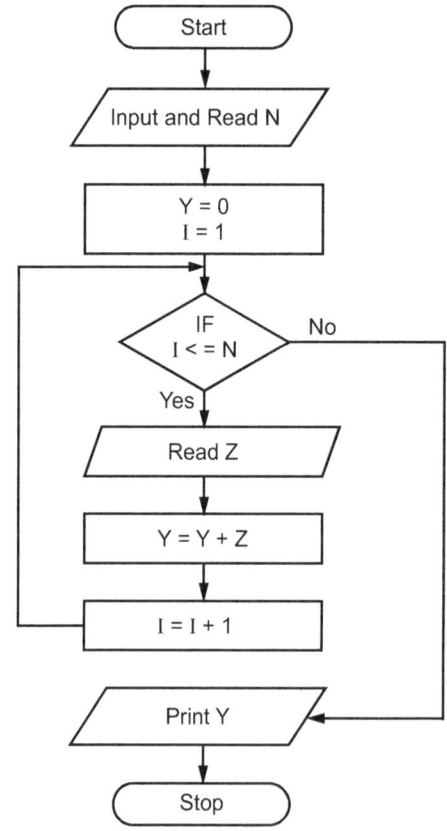

2.1.9 Reversing the Digits

- If there is a number 532, then the reverse of the digits of this number is 235.

Algorithm:

- **Step 1:** Start
- **Step 2:** Input and Read Num
- **Step 3:** R = 0, Rev = 0
- **Step 4:** R = Num % 10
  Rev = Rev * 10 + R
  Num = Num/10
- **Step 5:** If (Num > 0) then Goto Step 3 Else
  Goto Step 6
- **Step 6:** Display 'Reverse Number', i.e. Rev
- **Step 7:** Stop.

Flowchart:

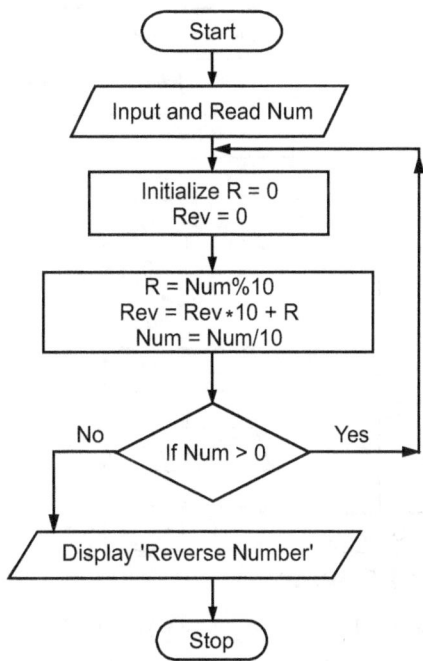

2.1.10 Generation of Table for a Given Number N

- If we have a number say 2 then we can generate the table of 2 such as,
  2*1=2
  2*2=4
  2*3=6
  2*4=8
  2*5=10
  ....:
  2*10=20

Algorithm:
- **Step 1:** Start
- **Step 2:** Input and Read M
- **Step 3:** I = 1
- **Step 4:** If (I < = 10) then
    Z = I * M
    Else Goto Step 7
- **Step 5:** Display Z
- **Step 6:** I = I + 1 Goto Step 4
- **Step 7:** Stop.

Flowchart:

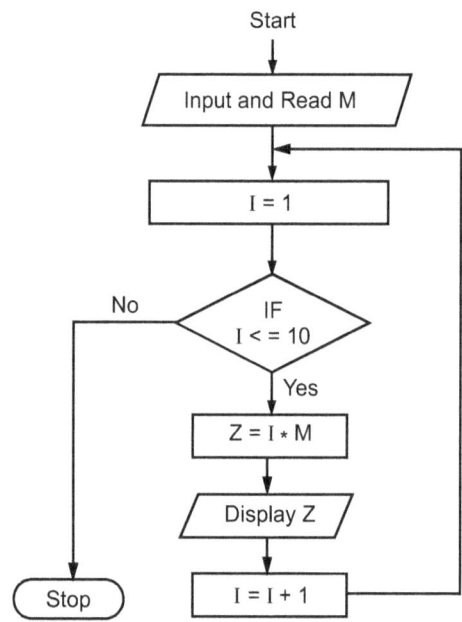

2.1.11 Computation of Power   (April 2015)

- It is a mathematical operation written as x^y. It involves two numbers, the base x and the exponent y.

Algorithm:
- **Step 1:** Start
- **Step 2:** Read and initialize x and y
- **Step 3:** Initialise a = 1, i=1
- **Step 4:** a=a*x; i=i+1
- **Step 5:** Repeat Step 4 till i<=y
- **Step 6:** Print a
- **Step 7:** Stop

Flowchart:

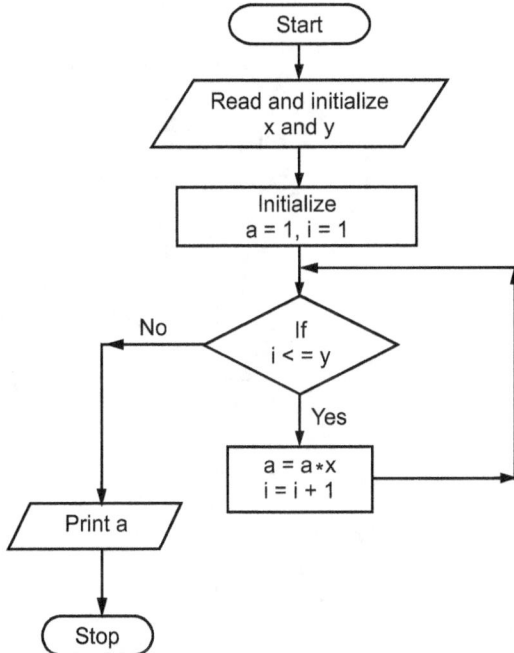

2.1.12 ^nC_r (Combinations)

- ^nC_r (combinations) is a method of selecting several items or symbols out of a larger group or a data set, where an order does not matter.
- Formula is,

$$^nC_r = \frac{n!}{r!\,(n-r)!}$$

Algorithm:

    Step 1: Start
    Step 2: Input and Read n, r
    Step 3: $a_1 = 1$, $a_2 = 1$, $a_3 = 1$, $^nC_r = 0$
    Step 4: For i = 1 to n in step of 1
              $a_1 = a_1 * i$
              i = i + 1
    Step 5: For i = 1 to r in Step of 1
              $a_2 = a_2 * i$
              i = i + 1
    Step 6: For i = 1 to (n – r) in step of 1
              $a_3 = a_3 * i$
              i = i + 1
    Step 7: $^nC_r = a_1 / (a_2 * a_3)$
    Step 8: Display ^nC_r
    Step 9: Stop

Flowchart:

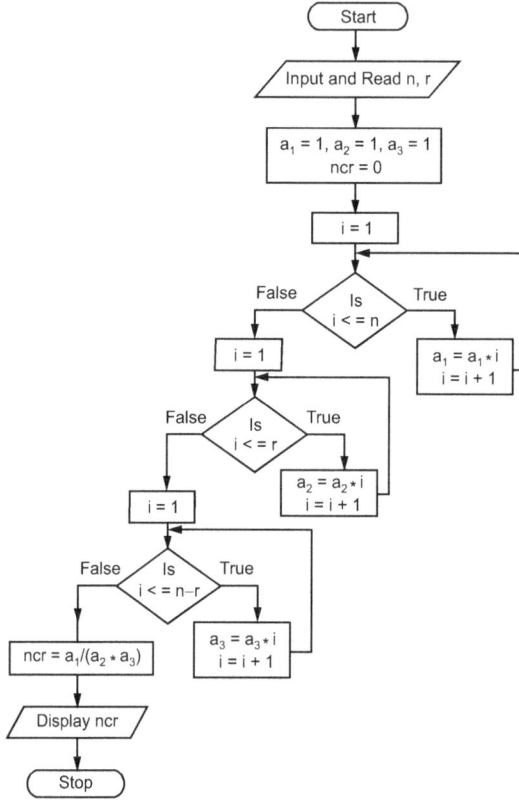

2.1.13 Pascal Triangle
- It is a triangular array of the binomial coefficients.
- Pascal's triangle is formed by starting with an apex of 1. In Pascal's triangle, every number below in the triangle is the sum of the two numbers diagonally above it to the left and the right, with positions outside the triangle counting as zero.

```
              1
           1     1
        1     2     1
     1     3     3     1
  1     4     6     4     1
```

Algorithm:
Step 1: Start
Step 2: Accept how many lines to print, i.e. r.
Step 3: Set i=0
Step 4: If i<r then Goto Step 5
Step 5: Set n=1
Step 6: Set k=i
Step 7: If k<r then print " "

Else Goto Step 9
Step 8: Increment k by 1
  i.e. k=k+1 Goto Step 7
Step 9: Set j=0
Step 10: If j<=i then
  print the value of n
  print " "
  calculate n=(n*(i−j)/(j+1))
  Else Goto Step 12
Step 11: Increment j by 1
  i.e. j=j+1 Goto Step 10
Step 12: Print newline
Step 13: Increment i by 1
  i.e. i=i+1
  Goto Step 4
Step 14: Stop

Flowchart:

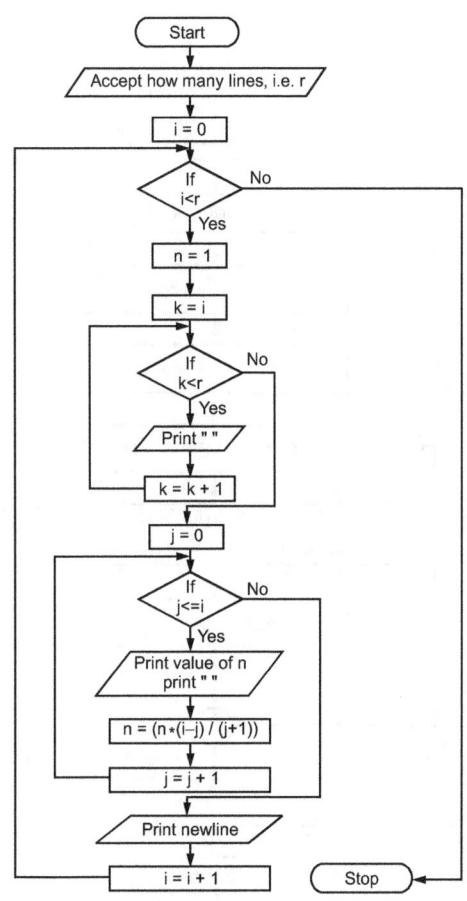

2.1.14 Sine Series

- Sin series is given by the following way:

$$\sin(x) = x - \frac{x^3}{3!} + \frac{x^5}{5!} \ldots\ldots$$

Algorithm:

Step 1: Start
Step 2: Read X and n
Step 3: Convert x values into radian using formula
X = X * 3.1412/180
Step 4: t = X
Step 5: Sum = X
Step 6: Step for loop from i = 1 until
(i < n + 1) increment 1
Step 7: t =(t*pow(double)(-1), (double) (2*i-1))*X*X)/(2*i*(2*i+1))
Step 8: Sum = sum + t
Step 9: Print sum
Step 10: Stop

Flowchart:

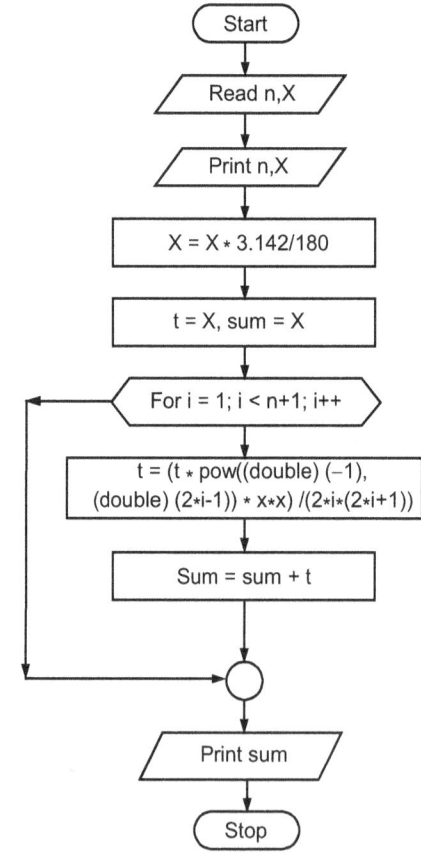

Description:
- Above and flowchart illustrate step for finding sine value of angle (x).
- Both algorithm and flowchart should have start and stop steps.
    Step 2: Read n, x as x = 45, n = 10
    Step 3: Print x and n, x = 45, n = 10
    Step 4: x = x * 3.142/180, x = 0.7855
    Step 5: t = x, sum = x
    Step 7: Calculating by formula provided in Step 7, for 10 time we get, sum = 0.71
    Step 8: Display sum = 0.71.
    Thus, we get value of sin(x) = sum, sin(45) = 0.71.

2.1.15 Cosine Series
- cos series is given by,

$$\cos(x) = 1 - \frac{x^2}{2!} + \ldots\ldots$$

Algorithm:
- **Step 1:** Start
- **Step 2:** Initialise n = 20;
- **Step 3:** Read X
- **Step 4:** Convert X values into radian using formula
    X = X * 3.142/180
- **Step 5:** t = 1, sum = 1
- **Step 6:** Set up loop from i = 1 until (i<n+1) increment
- **Step 7:** t = (t*(pow(double) (–1), (double) (2 * i – 1)) X * X/(2 * i * (2 *i – 1))
- **Step 8:** sum = sum + t
- **Step 9:** Display sum
- **Step 10:** Stop

Flowchart:

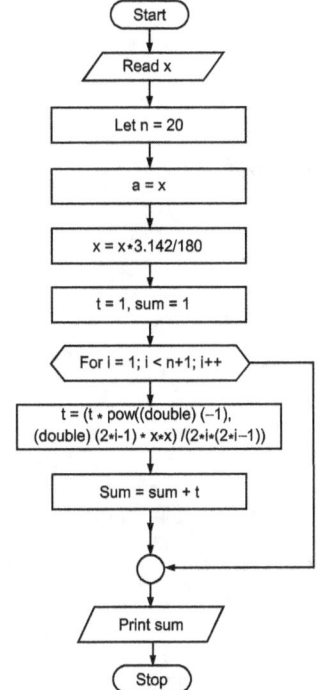

Description:

- Above algorithm and flowchart illustrate steps for finding cosine value of angle (x).
- Both algorithm and flowchart should have start and stop steps.

   Step 2: Read x. x as 60.

   Step 5: x = x * 3.142/180. x = 1.0473333

   Step 8: Calculating by formula provided in Step 8 for 20 times we get, sum = 0.500113

   Step 9: Display sum = 0.500113

   Thus, we get cosine of 60 = 0.500113.

2.1.16 Prime Numbers   (April 2015)

- In general, prime numbers are the numbers that are bigger than one (1) and cannot divide evenly by any other number except 1 and itself.
- For example, number 7 can only be divided evenly by 1 or 7. So it is a prime number, while 8 can be divided by 1, 2, 4 so it is not prime number.

   Step 1: Start

   Step 2: Read number n

   Step 3: X = 2; flag = true

   Step 4: If nMODx=0

   then flag=false, Goto Step 8.

   Step 5: X = X + 1

   Step 6: If x < n Goto Step 4

   Step 7: If flag = true then

   Print "Number is prime"

   Otherwise Goto Step 9

   Step 8: If flag=false, then

   Print "Number is not prime"

   Step 9: Stop.

Flowchart:

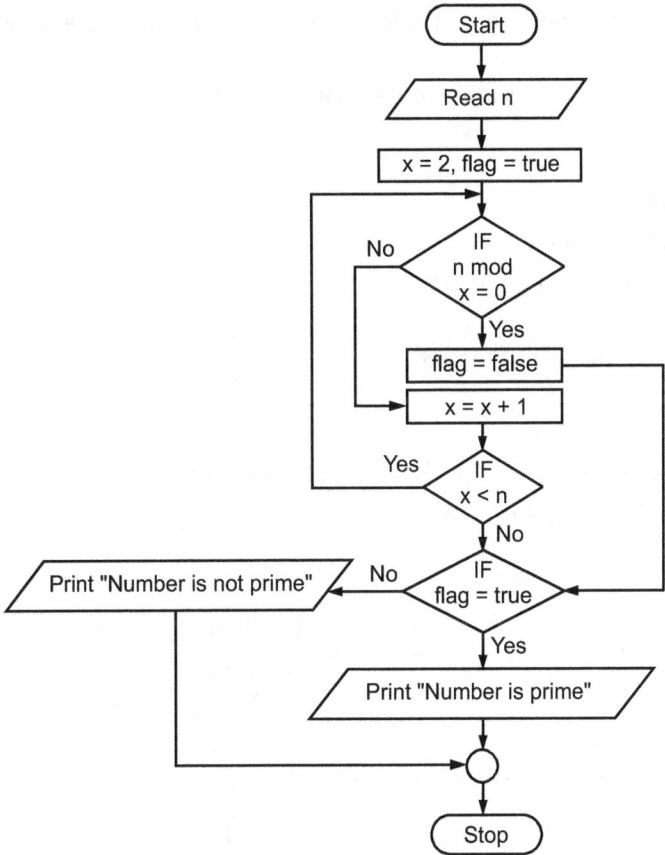

Description:

- The above algorithm and flowchart illustrate the steps for finding whether given number is prime or not.
- Both algorithm and flowchart should have start and stop steps.

  Step 2: Read n, n = 5

  Step 3: X=2, flag=true

  Step 4: 5 mod 2≠0

  Step 5: X=2+1=3

  Step 6: 3<5

  Now, steps 4, 5 and 6 are repeated till X = 5.

  Step 7: Flag = true as 5 is not divisible by 2, 3, 4.

  Step 8: Display number is prime.

2.1.17 Factors of a Number (Oct. 2014)

- The factors of a number are all those numbers that can divide evenly into the number with no remainder.
- For example, 12 is the factor of 48 because 12 divide exactly into 48 (48/12 = 4 i.e. no remainder).

Algorithm:
- **Step 1:** Start
- **Step 2:** Read a number, N
- **Step 3:** If N <= 0, then go to Step 8
- **Step 4:** Set i = 1
- **Step 5:** If i > N, then Goto Step 8
  Else
  Divide N by i
- **Step 6:** If the remainder of the division is zero then Print i
- **Step 7:** Increment i by 1 and Goto Step 5.
- **Step 8:** Stop.

Flowchart:

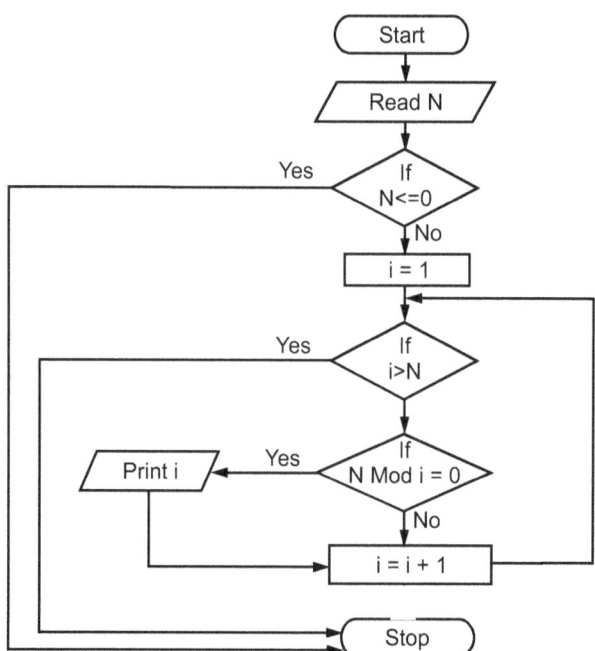

2.1.18 Perfect Number

- A perfect number is a positive integer where the sum of all its positive divisors, except itself, is equal to the number itself.
- For example, take number 6, because 1, 2, and 3 are its proper positive divisors, and 1 + 2 + 3 = 6. Hence, 6 is perfect number.

Algorithm:

Step 1: Start
Step 2: Accept the value of Num
Step 3: Initialize total=0, i=1
Step 4: If i<Num then Goto Step 5
Else Goto Step 7
Step 5: If Num % i=0 then increment total by 1 i.e. total=total+1
Step 6: Increment i by 1, i.e. i=i+1
Goto Step 4
Step 7: If total=Num then display "Num is a perfect number"
Else display 'Num is not a perfect number"
Step 8: Stop.

Flowchart:

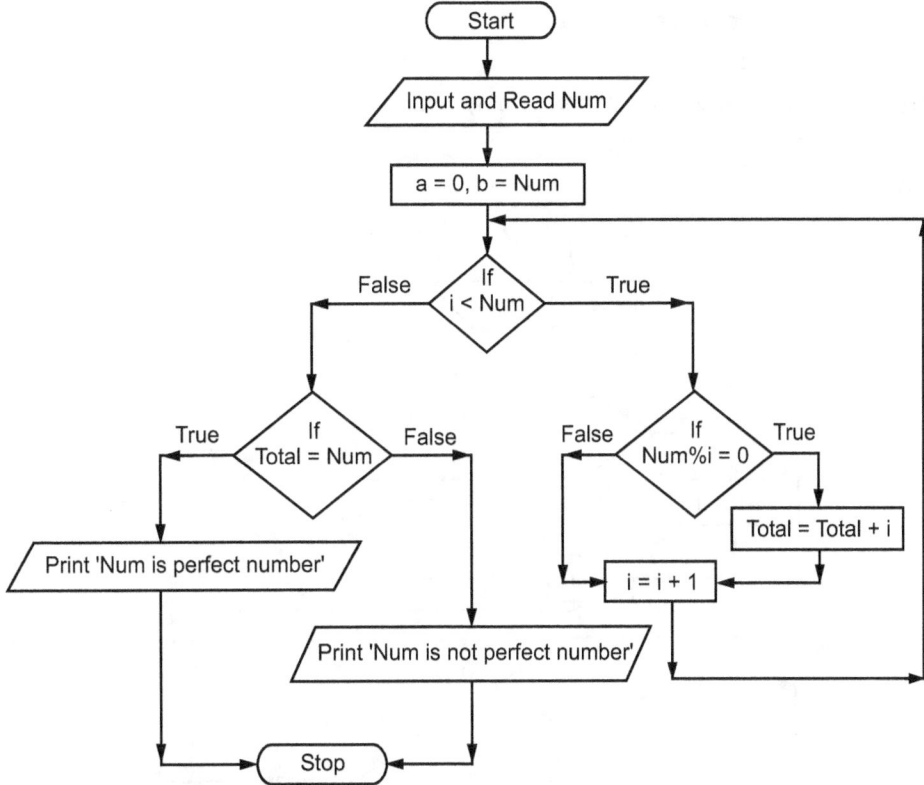

2.1.19 GCD of Two Numbers

- HCF (Highest Common Factor) also called as Greatest Common Divisor (GCD).
- GCD of two or more numbers is the greatest number that can exactly divide each one of the number.

- For example, the GCD of 4 and 12 is computed as follows,
    4 = 2 × 2
    12 = 2 × 2 × 3
  The GCD of 5 and 12 is 4 (i.e. 2 × 2)

Algorithm:

Step 1: Start

Step 2: Input and Read a, b

Step 3: If (a > b)
    max = b
    else
    max = a

Step 4: i=max

Step 5: if(i>=1) then
    Goto Step 6 Else
    Goto Step 7

Step 6: if(a%i=0 and b%i=0) then display "GCD is i"
    Else i=i−1 Goto Step 5

Step 7: Stop

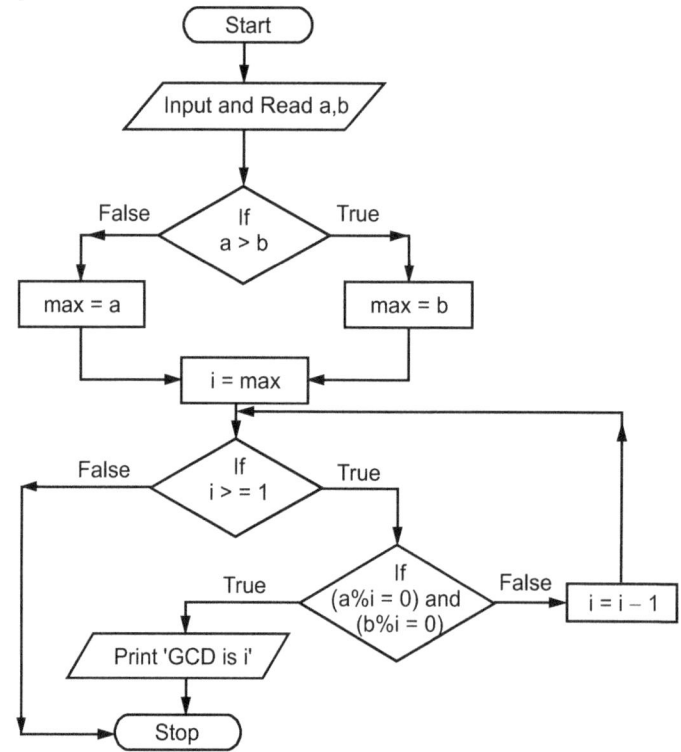

2.1.20 Factorial of a Number (Oct. 2014, April 2015)

- Following algorithm and flowchart shows step by step process to calculate a factorial of given number.

Algorithm:

Step 1: Start
Step 2: Read 'N'
Step 3: Fact=1, Counter=0
Step 4: Counter=counter+1
Step 5: If(counter<=N) then
  Fact=Fact*Counter
  Goto Step 4
Step 6: Display fact
Step 7: Stop

Flowchart:

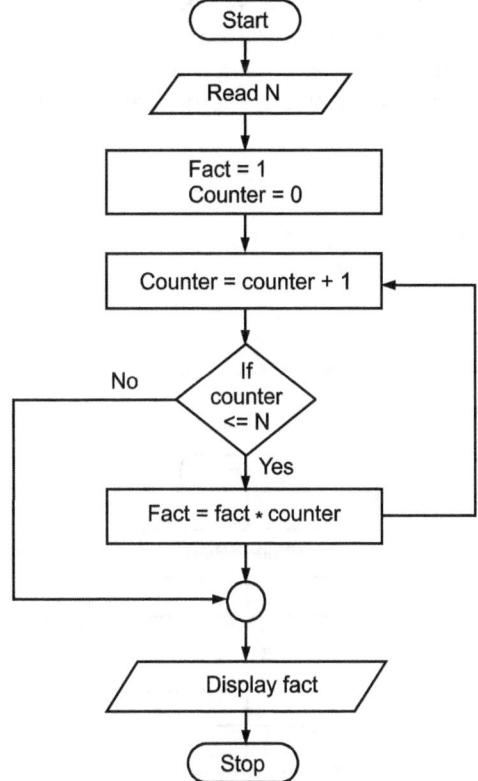

Description:
  Algorithm and flowchart illustrate steps to calculate factorial of a number.
  Both algorithm and flowchart should have start and stop steps.
  Step 2:   Read N = 3
  Step 3:   fact=1, counter=0
  Step 4:   counter=counter+1
  Step 5:   counter<=3
  ∴ fact=1*1
  Goto Step 4
  counter=2
  Again Step 5: counter<=3
  ∴ fact=1*2=2
  Goto Step 4: counter=3
  ∴ fact=2*3=6
  Goto Step 4: counter=4
  Step 5:   counter>N
  Hence Goto Step 6
  ∴ Display 6.

2.1.21 Other Algorithms and Flowcharts

1. Swapping two numbers using third variable.
- Swapping using third variable can be finding out by the ways of first store the number a to temp variable, next store the number a and b, after that store temp variable to a.
- Now numbers have been swapped.

Algorithm:
  Step 1: Start
  Step 2: Input and Read a, b
  Step 3: n = a
  Step 4: a = b
  Step 5: b = n
  Step 6: Print a, b
  Step 7: Stop

Flowchart:

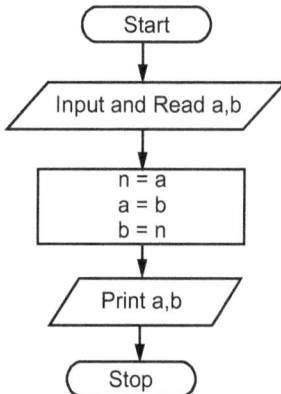

2. **Algorithm and flowchart to exchange the values of 2 variables A and B without using third temporary variable.**

   Algorithm:
   Step 1: Start
   Step 2: Read A and B
   Step 3: A = A + B
   Step 4: B = A − B
   Step 5: A = A − B
   Step 6: Display A, B
   Step 7: Stop

   Flowchart:

   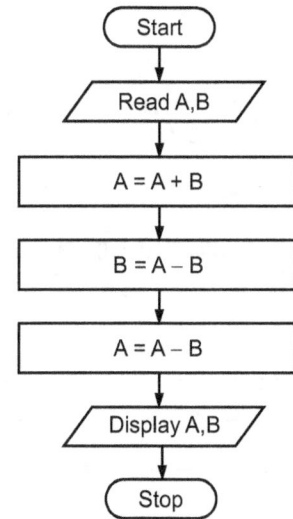

Description:
- Above algorithm and flowchart illustrates the steps for solving a problem of program for exchange the values of 2 variables A and B without using third temporary variable.
- Both the algorithm and flowchart should always have a start at the beginning.

   Step 2: Read A and B as
   A = 15, B = 30
   Step 3: Calculate A = A + B,
   A = 45
   Step 4: Calculate B = A − B,
   B = 15 (45 − 30)
   Step 5: Calculate A = A − B,
   A = 30 (45 − 15)
   Step 6: Display A and B,
   A = 30, B = 15

3. To check leap year or not. (Oct. 2014)

- A year will be said leap year if it is divisible by 4 but not by 100 or it is divisible by 400.

Algorithm:

Step 1: Start
Step 2: Input and Read year
Step 3: If((year%4=0) and (year%100≠0)) OR (Year%400=0))
   Print "Leap year"
   Else
   Print "Not leap year"
Step 4: Stop

Flowchart:

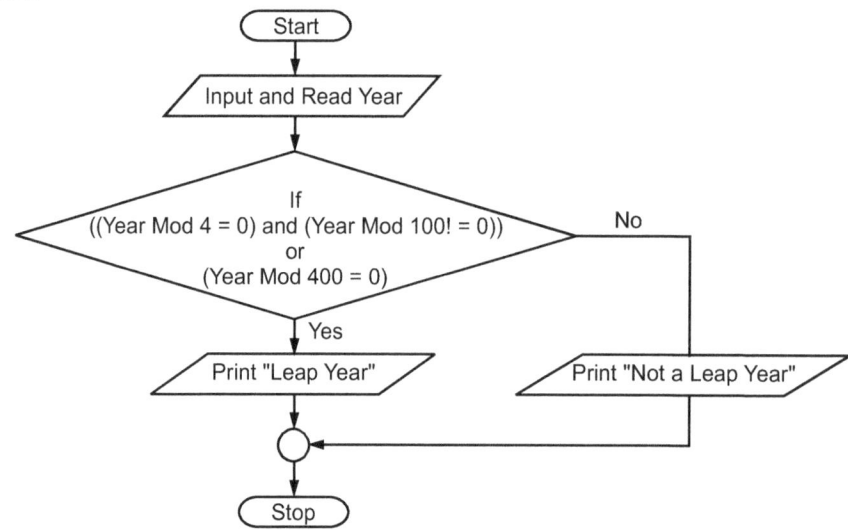

4. Algorithm and flowchart to check palindrome: (Oct. 2014)

- A palindrome is a word whose meaning may be interpreted the same way in either forward or reverse direction.
- A palindrome number is a number that remains the same when its digits are reversed. For example, number 12421 is "symmetrical", hence it is palindrome.

Algorithm:

Step 1: Start
Step 2: Input and Read Num
Step 3: a = 0, b = Num
Step 4: While (Num > 0)
   r = Num%10
   Num = Num/10
   a = a*10/r

Step 5: If (b = a)
  Print 'Number is Palindrome'
else
  Print 'Number is Not Palindrome'
Step 6: Stop

Flowchart:

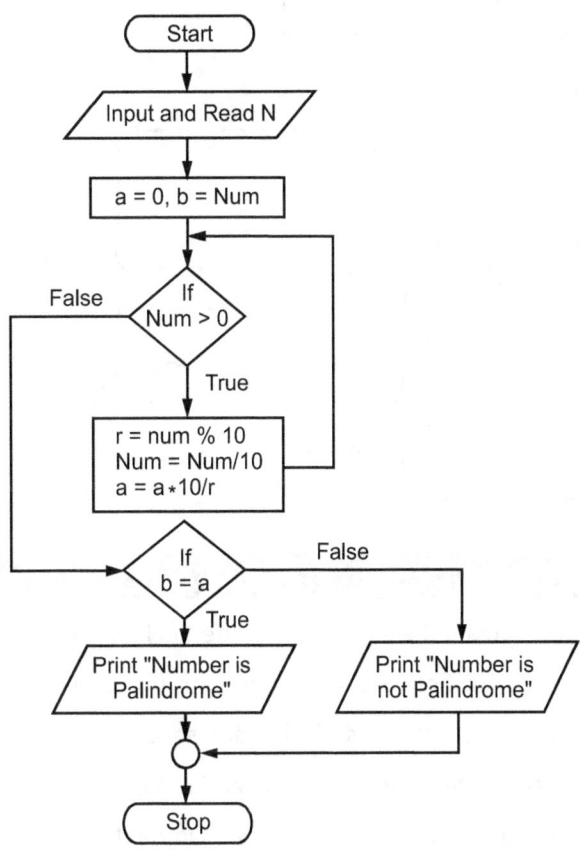

5. Algorithm and flowchart for sum of digits. (April 2015)
- Sum of digits of given number means if number is 2345, then sum is 2 + 3 + 4 + 5 = 14.

Algorithm:
  Step 1: Start
  Step 2: Input number as X
  Step 3: a = 0
  Step 4: If X > 0 then repeat Steps 4 through 7
  Step 5: b = X%10
  Step 6: a = a + b
  Step 7: X = X/10
  Step 8: Print a
  Step 9: Stop

Flowchart:

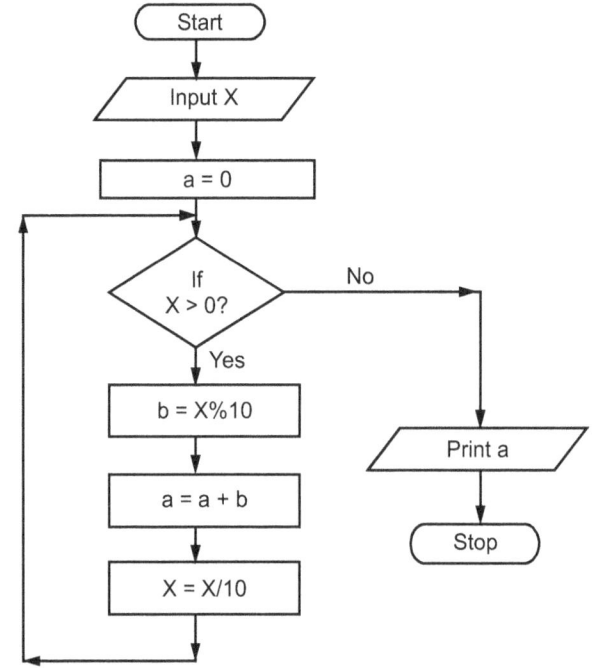

Questions

1. Draw a flowchart to calculate the sum and average of N numbers.
2. Draw a flowchart to check whether a given number is prime or not.
3. Draw a flowchart to generate N terms of Fibonacci series.
4. Draw a flowchart to calculate x^n where x is real and n is an integer.
5. Draw a flowchart to find all divisors of an integer number N.
6. Accept the day of the week and display whether the day is a 'Working Day' or 'Week End'. Display proper 'Error Message' for all incorrect inputs.
7. Write an algorithm and draw a flowchart to check whether the given string is palindrome or not.
8. Write an algorithm and flowchart for university system.
9. Write an algorithm and flowchart for insurance company.
10. Draw flowchart for library management system.

University Questions and Answers

October 2014

1. What is palindrome? [2M]

   Ans. Please refer to Section 2.1.21 Point (4).

2. Write an algorithm for factorial of a given number. [4M]

   Ans. Please refer to Section 2.1.20.

3. Write an algorithm to print factors of a given number. [4M]

   Ans. Please refer to Section 2.1.17.

4. Draw a flow chart to find the given year is leap year or not. [4M]

   Ans. Please refer to Section 2.1.21 Point (3).

5. Draw a flow chart for sum of first n natural numbers. [4M]

   Ans. Please refer to Section 2.1.7.

6. Draw a flow chart for multiplication of 2 numbers. [4M]

   Ans. Please refer to Section 2.1.2.

April 2015

1. What is factorial number? [2M]

   Ans. Please refer to Section 2.1.20.

2. Draw a flowchart to calculate sum of digits of given number. [4M]

   Ans. Please refer to Section 2.1.21 Point (5).

3. Write an algorithm to find given number is prime or not. [4M]

   Ans. Please refer to Section 2.1.16.

4. Draw a flowchart to calculate x^y. [4M]

   Ans. Please refer to Section 2.1.11.

5. Draw a flowchart to find maximum of three numbers. [4M]

   Ans. Please refer to Section 2.1.6.

6. Write an algorithm to find sum of 'n' given numbers. [4M]

   Ans. Please refer to Section 2.1.8.

7. Write an algorithm to calculate netpay=basic+DA+HRA for given basic and DA is 80%, HRA is 20%, is PF 25% of basic. [4M]

Ans.

Step 1 : Start

Step 2 : Read Basic

Step 3 : Calculate DA=Basic*0.8

Step 4 : Calculate HRA=Basic*0.2

Step 5 : Calculate PF=Basic*0.25

Step 6 : Calculate NetPay=Basic+DA+HRA-PF

Step 7 : Stop

✱✱✱

Chapter 3...

Recursion

Contents ...

3.1 Concept

    3.1.1 Definition

    3.1.2 Recursive Algorithm

    3.1.3 Types of Recursion

    3.1.4 Advantages and Disadvantages

3.2 Multiplication

3.3 Factorial

3.4 Ackermann Function

3.5 Fibonacci Series

3.6 Permutation Generation

- Questions
- University Questions and Answers

3.1 Concept (Oct. 2014)

- Recursion is an important and powerful tool in problem solving and programming. It is a programming technique that naturally implements the divide-and-conquer problem solving methodology.

- Recursion refers to the concept of a thing repeating within itself. Recursion can be used as an alternative to iteration.

- Recursion is a function invoking itself, either directly or indirectly.

- Recursive functions are very useful to solve mathematical problems such as finding factorial of a number, generating Fibonacci series etc. Recursion can be used to replace complex nesting code by dividing the problem into same problem of its sub-type.

- Every recursive function must have a termination condition, otherwise it will run infinite times.

3.1.1 Definition (Oct. 2014)

- We can define recursion as "defining a problem in terms of itself".

OR

- Recursion is a method of solving problems that involves breaking a problem down into smaller and smaller subproblems itself until you get to a small enough problem that it can be solved trivially.

3.1.2 Recursive Algorithm (Oct. 2014)

- An algorithm is said to be recursive or employ recursion when it calls itself during execution. Usually, the algorithm will call itself using a smaller version of the original input.
- In recursive algorithm the problem is break or split into one or more simplex versions of itself.
- Recursive algorithms solve the problem by solving smaller versions of the problem:
  - If the smaller versions are only a little smaller, the algorithm can be called a reduce and conquer algorithm.
  - If the smaller versions are about half the size of the original, the algorithm can be called a divide and conquer algorithm

3.1.3 Types of Recursion (Oct. 2014)

- The class of recursive algorithms is divided into following subclasses.

1. Linear Recursion:

- In the recursion, only one internal recursive call is made within the body of the function. In this a function call itself in a simple manner and by termination condition it stops execution.
- This is known as 'winding' and when it returns to caller is called as 'unwinding'. The termination condition is called as Base condition.

Winding steps:

Function called	Function return
fact(6)	6*fact(5)
fact(5)	5*fact(4)
fact(4)	4*fact(3)
fact(3)	3*fact(2)
fact(2)	2*fact(1)
fact(1)	1*fact(0)

fact(0) is terminating point as it returns 1.

Unwinding steps:

It works in reverse order as compared to winding steps.

fact(1)	1*1
fact(2)	2*1
fact(3)	3*2*1
fact(4)	4*3*2*1
fact(5)	5*4*3*2*1
fact(6)	6*5*4*3*2*1

2. **Binary Recursion:**
- A function that makes two recursive calls to itself is said to use binary recursion.
- A problem is solved by first dividing it into two smaller problems that are in turn solved by being divided into two smaller problems, and so on recursively.
- Simple example of this type is generating n^{th} Fibonacci number.

```
int fibnumber(int n)
{
    // Base conditions
    if(n<1)
        return -1;
    if(n==1 || n==2)
        return 1;
    // Recursive call twice
        return fibnumber (n-1) + fibnumber (n-2);
    // At a time two recursive function
    // called, hence it is binary
}
```

3. **Non-linear Recursion:**
- When a function uses a number of internal recursive calls within the body of the function, then the function is said to have non-linear recursion.
- In this, a number of internal recursive calls are usually generated by embedding a single recursive call within a loop.
- The format of such non-linear recursive function is given below.

```
type nonlinear (...)
{
```

```
        for(i=k; i<n; i++)
        {
            statements or actions
            if(termination condition not met)
                recursive call to nonlinear
            else
                statements or actions
        }
    }
```
where 'type' is the return type of function.

4. **Mutual Recursion:**
- In this type, two functions call each other. In a sense, the two (or more) functions are engaged with each other together.
- The format of such mutual recursion is given below.

```
    type first(…)
    {
        .
        .
        .
        internal call to second
        .
        .
        .
    }
    type second (…)
    {
        .
        .
        .
        internal call to first
        .
        .
        .
    }
```
where 'type' is the return type of function.

3.1.4 Advantages and Disadvantages

Advantages: (April 2015)
1. Usually simplicity and easy.
2. The recursion is very flexible.
3. Using recursion, the length of the program can be reduced.

Disadvantages
1. It requires extra storage space.
2. Often the algorithm may require large amounts of memory if the depth of the recursion is very large. If the programmer forgets to specify the exit condition in the recursive function, the program will execute out of memory.
3. Inefficient in terms of execution speed and time.
4. Some function calls inside recursion are repeated or duplicated just like Fibonacci.

3.2 Multiplication

- Multiplication operation can be simulated as repetitive (recursive) addition of a number.
- The recursive definition of multiplying two numbers say a and b as given below :

$$\text{Multiply }(a, b) = \begin{cases} a & , \text{If } b = 1 \\ a + \text{Multiply }(a, b-1) & , \text{Otherwise} \end{cases}$$

Algorithm:

Step 1: Start

Step 2: Input (Accept) two numbers i.e. first and second

Step 3: Sum = 0, Index variable, i = 0.

Step 4: If i < abs (second)
then
sum=sum + abs (first),
Else
Goto Step 6

Step 5: Increment index variable value by 1
i = i + 1 Goto Step 4

Step 6: If both numbers are either positive or negative
Print sum with negative sign
Else
Print sum with positive sign

Step 7: Stop

Flowchart:

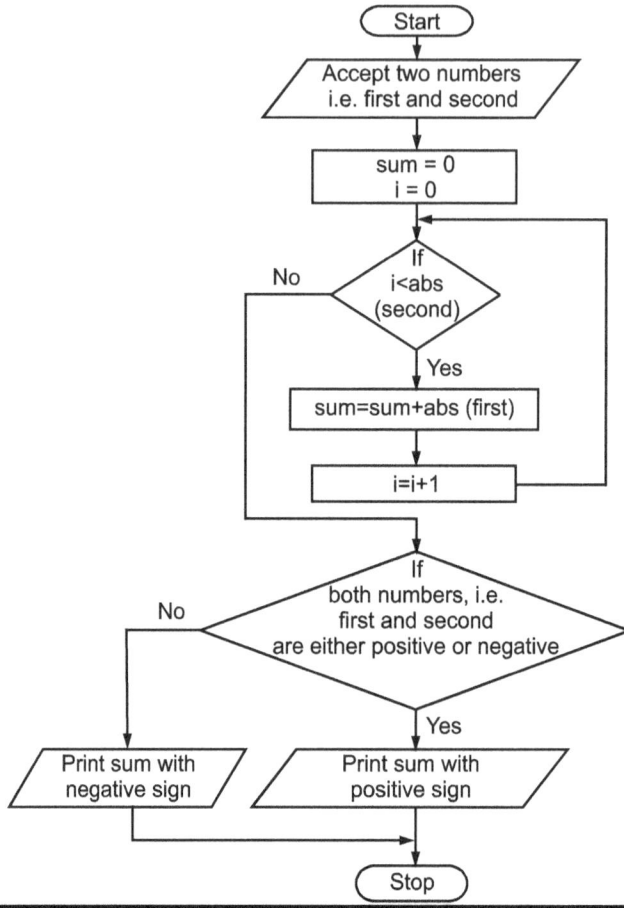

3.3 Factorial

- Factorial n (n!) is the product of positive integers from 1 to n.
- The definition of n! is as given below.

    n! = 1*2*3*4* ...*(n−1)*n, for n≥1

    We also know that,

    0!=1

    By applying factorial definition we get,

    0!=1
    1!=1*1
    2!=1*2
    3!=1*2*3
    .
    .
    .

- We observe that 3! contains all the factors of 2!. Only we have added number 3 in 3!. Hence, n! can always be calculated from (n−1)!

  n!=n*(n−1)!, for n≥1

  Using this we can rewrite above terms as,

  1!=1*0!
  2!=2*1!
  3!=3*2!
  .
  .
  .

- Recursive definition of factorial can be given below:

  Factorial (0) = 1,   n = 0

  Factorial (n) = n * factorial (n − 1) for n > 0.

  Algorithm for Factorial: A generalised description of algorithm for factorial of a number is given below.

  1. Treat 0! as a special case (0!=1).
  2. Compute each of the 'n' remaining products from its predecessor by use of recursion.
  3. Display the result, which is the value of n factorial.

- The program for finding the factorial of a number using recursion is as follows.

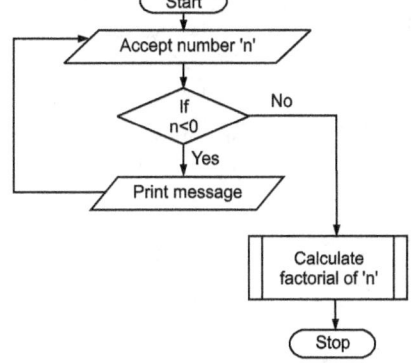

Subprocess :

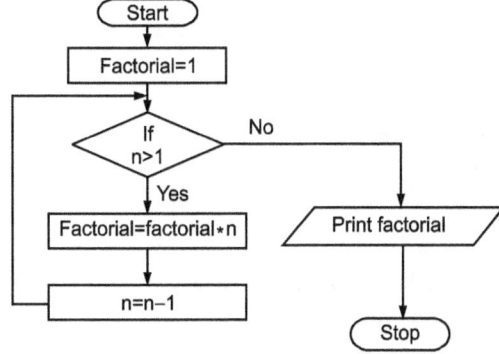

3.4 Ackermann Function

- It is a function with two arguments each of which can be assigned any non-negative integer – 0, 1, 2, 3, ……
- Ackermann's function A(m, n) is defined as follows:

$$A(m, n) = \begin{cases} n+1 & \text{if } m=0 \\ A(m-1, 1) & \text{if } m>0 \text{ and } n=0 \\ A(m-1, A(m, n-1)) & \text{if } m>0 \text{ and } n>0 \end{cases}$$

- Small portion of table showing Ackermann function values

m\n	0	1	2	3	…	N
0	1	2	3	4	…	n+1
1	2	3	4	5	…	n+2
2	3	5	7	9	…	2n+3
3	5	13	29	61	…	2(n+3)-3

Process Name : Ack

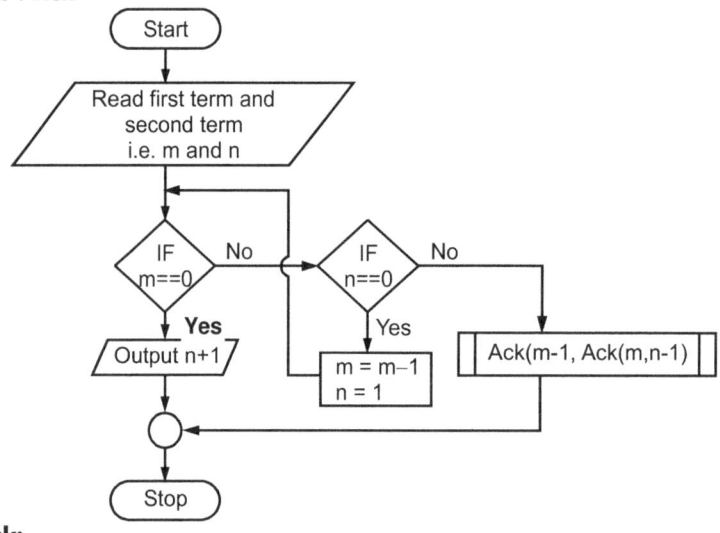

Algorithm Ack:
    Step 1: Start
    Step 2: Read first and second term, i.e. m and n
    Step 3: If m is equal to zero then
        output n+1
        Goto Step 5
        Else
        Goto Step 4
    Step 4: If n is equal to zero then
        m=m–1
        n=1
        Goto Step 3
        Else
        recursively call algorithm Ack as follows
        Ack(m–1,Ack(m,n–1))
    Step 5: Stop

The previous algorithm is traced with the following inputs.
1. m=2, n=2
As m and n are greater than zero, algorithm will call itself recursively as follows.
Ack(m-1, Ack(m,n-1)) = Ack(2,2)=Ack(1, Ack(2,1)) →1
Inner function call (underlined) will be executed first. As m and n are greater than zero, algorithm will call itself recursively as follows.
　　　Ack(2,1)=Ack(1, Ack(2,0)) →2
Inner function call (underlined) will be executed first. Here, m=2 and n=0.
At Step 4, m=m-1=1 and n=1 Goto Step 3. Again, m and n are greater than zero, i.e. Else of Step 4, algorithm will call itself recursively as follows.
Ack(2,0)=Ack(0, Ack(1,0)) →3
Inner function call (underlined) will be executed first. Here, m=1 and n=0. At Step 4, m=0, n=1 Goto Step 3. Now, m is equal to zero. Hence, n+1=2 is substituted for the Ack(1,0) in equation 3.
Hence, equation 3 now becomes Ack(2,0)=Ack(0,2). At Step 3, m==0. Hence, n+1=3 is substituted for Ack(2,0) at equation 2. So, equation 2 becomes Ack(2,1)=Ack(1,3)
At equation 2, Ack(2,1)=Ack(1,3)
Again, m and n are greater than zero, i.e. Else of Step 4, algorithm will call itself recursively as follows.
Ack(1,3)=Ack(0,Ack(1,2)) → 4
Inner function call (underlined) will be executed first. Again, m and n are greater than zero, i.e. Else of Step 4, algorithm will call itself recursively as follows.
Ack(1,2)=Ack(0, Ack(1,1)) → 5
Inner function call (underlined) will be executed first. Again, m and n are greater than zero, i.e. Else of Step 4, algorithm will call itself recursively as follows.
Ack(1,1)=Ack(0, Ack(1,0)) → 6
Inner function call (underlined) will be executed first. At Step 4, m=m-1=0 and n=1. Goto Step 3.
Now, m is equal to zero. Hence, n+1=2 is substituted for the Ack(1,0) in equation 6.
Hence, equation 6 now becomes Ack(1,1)=Ack(0,2). At Step 3, m=0. Hence, n+1=3 is substituted for Ack(1,1) in equation 5. So, equation 5 becomes Ack(1,2)=Ack(0,3)
At Step 3, m=0. Hence, n+1=4 is substituted for Ack(1,2) in equation 4.
Hence, equation 4 now becomes Ack(1,3)=Ack(0,4).
At Step 3, m=0. Hence, n+1=5 is substituted for Ack(1,3) in equation 2.
Hence, equation 2 now becomes Ack(2,1)=5.
The value of Ack(2,1) is substituted in equation 1 which now becomes,
Ack(2,2)=Ack(1,5) → 7
Here, m and n are greater than zero, i.e. Else of Step 4, algorithm will call itself recursively as follows.
Ack(1,5)=Ack(0, Ack(1,4)) → 8
Inner function call (underlined) will be executed first. Again, m and n are greater than zero, i.e. Else of Step 4, algorithm will call itself recursively as follows.
Ack(1,4)=Ack(0, Ack(1,3)) → 9
Inner function call (underlined) will be executed first. Again, m and n are greater than zero, i.e. Else of Step 4, algorithm will call itself recursively as follows.
Ack(1,3)=Ack(0, Ack(1,2)) → 10
Inner function call (underlined) will be executed first. Again, m and n are greater than zero, i.e. Else of Step 4, algorithm will call itself recursively as follows.

Ack(1,2)=Ack(0, Ack(1,1)) → 11
Inner function call (underlined) will be executed first. Again, m and n are greater than zero, i.e. Else of Step 4, algorithm will call itself recursively as follows.
Ack(1,1)=Ack(0, Ack(1,0)) → 12
Inner function call (underlined) will be executed first. Here, m=1 and n=0. At Step 4, m=m-1=0 and n=1. Goto Step 3. At Step 3, m==0. Hence, output n+1=2, i.e. Ack(1,0)=2, which is substituted in equation 12.
Hence, Ack(1,1)=Ack(0,2). At Step 3, m==0. Therefore, output n+1=3, i.e. Ack(0,2)=3, which is substituted in equation 11.
Hence, Ack(1,2)=Ack(0,3). At Step 3, m==0. Therefore, output n+1=4, i.e. Ack(0,3)=4, which is substituted in equation 10.
Hence, Ack(1,3)=Ack(0,4). At Step 3, m==0. Therefore, output n+1=5, i.e. Ack(0,4)=5, which is substituted in equation 9.
Hence, Ack(1,4)=Ack(0,5). At Step 3, m==0. Therefore, output n+1=6, i.e. Ack(0,5)=6, which is substituted in equation 8.
Hence, Ack(1,5)=Ack(0,6). At Step 3, m==0. Therefore, output n+1=7, i.e. Ack(0,6)=7, which is substituted in equation 7.
Hence, Ack(2,2)=7
2. m=1 and n=1
As m and n are greater than zero, algorithm will call itself recursively as follows.
Ack(m-1, Ack(m,n-1)) = Ack(1,1)=Ack(0, Ack(1,0)) → 1
Inner function call (underlined) will be executed first. Here, m=1 and n=0. At Step 4, m=0, n=1 Goto Step 3. Now, m is equal to zero. Hence, n+1=2 is substituted for the Ack(1,0) in equation 1.
Equation 1 now becomes, Ack(1,1)=Ack(0,2). At Step 3, m==0. Therefore, output n+1=3,i.e.Ack(0,2)=3, equation 1 now becomes, Ack(1,1)=Ack(0,2)=3
Hence, Ack(1,1)=3

3.5 Fibonacci Series (April 2015)

- Leonardo Fibonacci discovered a simple numerical series called Fibonacci Series. Starting with 0 and 1, each new number in the series is simply the sum of the two numbers before it.
- The first few terms of Fibonacci series are:
  0, 1, 1, 2, 3, 5, 8, 13, ...
- Fibonacci numbers have a property that the ratio of two consecutive numbers tends to the Golden Ratio as numbers get bigger and bigger.
- The Golden Ratio is a number and it happens to be approximately 1.618.

Algorithm:
Start 1: Start
Step 2: Accept n, the number of fibonacci terms to be generated.
Step 3: Initialize first two fibonacci numbers, namely a and b.
Step 4: Initialise count of number generated.
Step 5: While less than 'n' fibonacci numbers are generated do
  (i) Print next two fibonacci numbers.
  (ii) Generate next fibonacci number keeping 'a' relevant.

(iii) Generate next fibonacci number from most recent pair keeping 'b' relevant for next computation.
(iv) Update the counter i.e. Fibonacci numbers generated.

Step 6: If n is even then print last two Fibonacci numbers.
Else print second last Fibonacci number.

Step 7: Stop.

Flowchart:

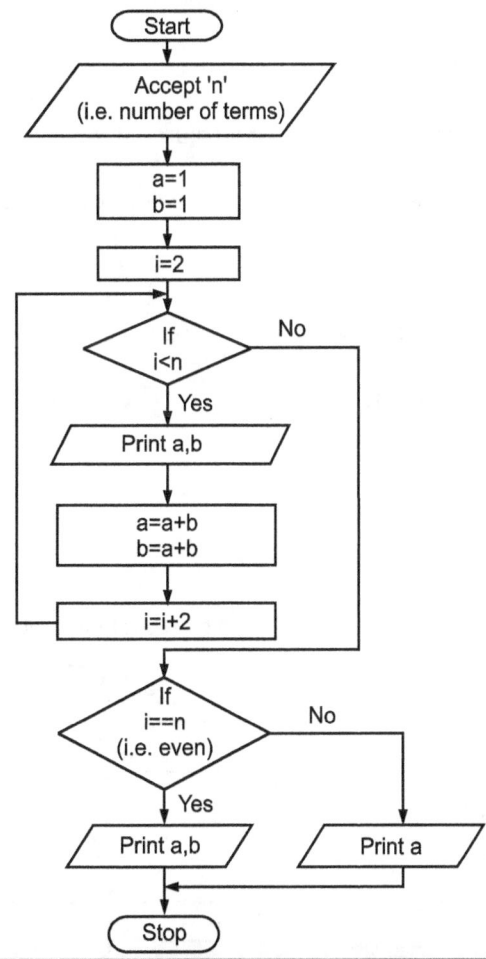

3.6 Permutation Generation

- Consider an example involving the generation of all permutations of the first 5 integers taken 3 at a time. Sequences like {1, 2, 3}, {2, 1, 3} and {3, 1, 2} are distinct permutations.
- Three things to remember about permutation sets are:
    1. Each column must be able to take on all of the first 'n' integer values.
    2. Integers in a permutation need not be ordered.
    3. There should be no repetitions within a given permutation.

Algorithm:

Step 1: Start

Step 2: Establish set size, permutation size, array for storing the permutations. Set index to current column of permutation set.

Step 3: While all available values for current column not selected do

    (i) Swap j^{th} value from unchosen set with current column value.

    (ii) If current column index not at final column then

        Recursively generate next column values by calling procedure.

    else

        new permutation is available, hence print it.

    (iii) Reverse the swappings done in (i).

Stop 4: Stop.

Flowchart:

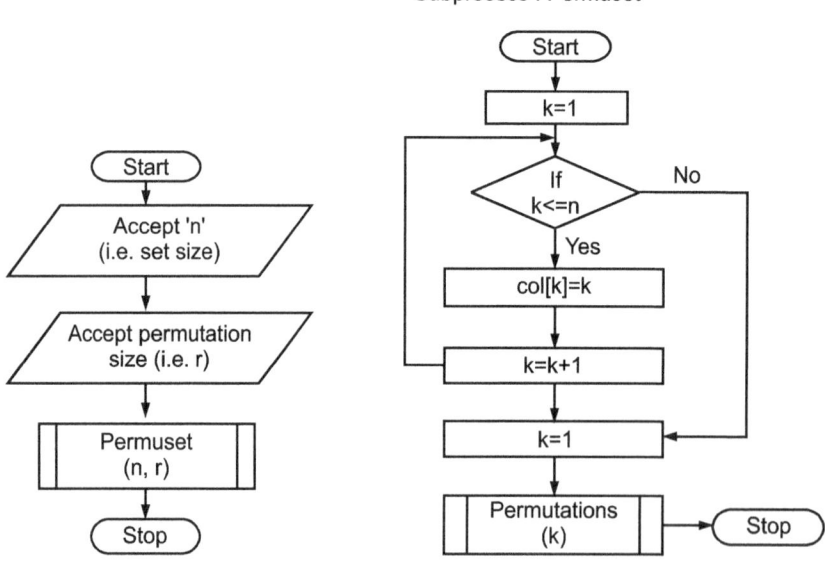

Sub process: Permutations

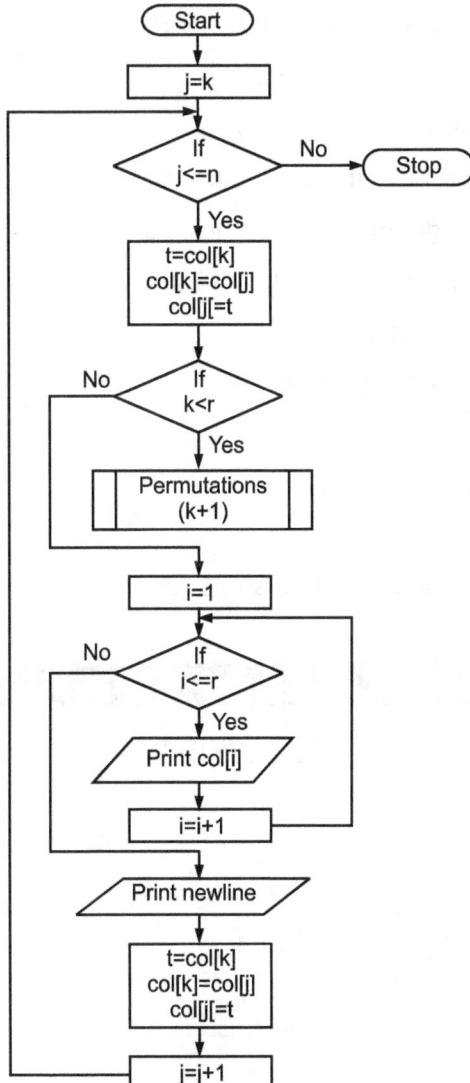

- **Permutations of a given string:** A string of length n has n! permutation. If the given string is ABC, then its permutations are: ABC, ACB, BAC, BCA, CAB, CBA.

Questions

1. What is recursion? Explain the subclasses of Recursion.
2. Define recursion.
3. What is binary recursion?

4. State the properties of recursion.

5. State the difference between linear and binary recursion.

6. Where ackermann's function can be used?

7. Define non-linear recursion.

8. List the important things about the permutation sets.

9. Trace the Ackermann's algorithm on following input m = 2, n = 1.

10. What is multiplication? Draw flowchart for multiplication.

11. What is meant by fibonacci series?

12. Write short note on: Permutation generation.

13. What is factorial?

14. Write algorithm and draw flowchart for:

    (i) Factorial, (ii) Fibonacci series.

15. Write algorithm for permutation. Also draw flowchart for it.

University Questions and Answers

October 2014

1. What is recursion? [2M]

Ans. Please refer to Sections 3.1 and 3.1.1.

2. Explain concept of recursion. [4M]

Ans. Please refer to Sections 3.1.2 and 3.1.3.

April 2015

1. Explain advantages of recursion. [4M]

Ans. Please refer to Section 3.1.4.

2. Write an algorithm to print Fibonacci series upto 'n' term. [4M]

Ans. Please refer to Section 3.5.

***

Chapter 4...

Algorithms Using Arrays

Contents ...

4.1 Introduction
    4.1.1 Definition
    4.1.2 Characteristics of Arrays
    4.1.3 Array Terminology
    4.1.4 Types of Arrays
    4.1.5 Advantages and Disadvantages

4.2 Maximum and Minimum of Arrays
    4.2.1 Reversing Elements of an Array

4.3 Mean and Median of n Numbers

4.4 Array Representation
    4.4.1 Row-major Form of Array Representation
    4.4.2 Column-major Form of Array Representation

4.5 Matrices
    4.5.1 Addition
    4.5.2 Matrix Multiplication
    4.5.3 Transpose of Matrix
    4.5.4 Matrix Symmetry
    4.5.5 Upper and Lower Triangular Matrix

- Questions
- University Questions and Answers

4.1 Introduction   (Oct. 2014, April 2015)

- Algorithm is a solution to a problem written in a step by step manner.
- An array is a sequenced collection of elements of the same data type. All the elements in an array have same size and data type.

- Array elements share common name and array elements are stored in sequential memory locations.
- The variable a is declared and a memory location of two bytes is allocated to it. Later, a single value can be stored in it as shown in Fig. 4.1.

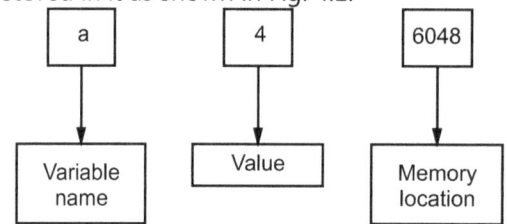

Fig. 4.1: Variable, value and address of a variable

4.1.1 Definition (April 2015)

- An array is a fixed number of similar type of elements (objects) which are stored in adjacent memory location.

OR

- An array is a sequence of data item of homogeneous value (same type).

OR

- An array is a finite collection of similar elements stored in adjacent memory locations.

4.1.2 Characteristics of Arrays

- Characteristics of Arrays as given below:
  1. An array holds elements that have the same data type.
  2. Array elements are stored in subsequent memory locations.
  3. Two-dimensional array elements are stored row by row in subsequent memory locations.
  4. Array name represents the address of the starting element.
  5. Array size should be mentioned in the declaration. Array size must be a constant expression and not a variable.

4.1.3 Array Terminology

- Array terminology are described below:
  1. **Rank:** The number of dimensions of an array is called its rank. A one-dimensional array has rank 1, a two-dimensional array has rank 2 and so on.
  2. **Bounds:** An array's bounds are the upper and lower limits of the index in each dimension.
  3. **Extent:** The number of elements along a dimension of an array is called the extent. For example,
     ```
     integer, dimension(-10:15):: Current
     ```
     has bounds −10 and 15 and an extent of 26.
  4. **Size:** The total number of elements in an array is its size.
  5. **Shape:** The shape of an array is determined by its rank and its extents in each dimension.

6. **Conformable:** Two arrays are said to be conformable if they have the same shape, that is, they have the same rank and the same extent in each dimension.
7. **Type:** It reflects to datatype like int, char, float, etc.

4.1.4 Types of Arrays (April 2015)

- Fig. 4.2 shows classification (types) of arrays.
- A one dimensional array is an array of values like {1, 2, 3}. A multi-dimensional array is an array of arrays like {{1, 2,}, {3, 4}, {5, 6}}.

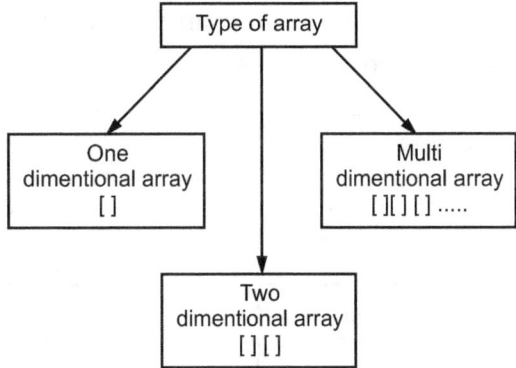

Fig. 4.2: Types of array

1. **One dimensional arrays or Single dimensional array or Linear array:**
- In one-dimensional arrays, each element in the array is referenced by a single subscript (index).
- In other words "for a one dimensional array we have a single index i.e. the array consists of only a single subscript".
- Single or one dimensional array is used to represent and store data in a linear form.
- For example, if we want to represent five numbers by an array variable, then we have to declare the variable 'n' as follows:
    ```
    int n[5];
    ```

Example:
```
a[0],a[1],a[2],a[3],..........a[n-1]
```
- It can be observed that total number of elements in above array is 'n'.
- An array can be declared in the following ways:
    ```
    int num[]={2,3,7,6,0};
    ```

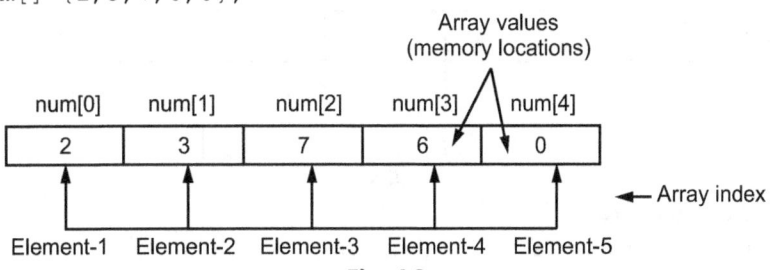

Fig. 4.3

- Here, we don't need to mention the size of the integer array since we are assigning the values to all the elements at the time of the declaration itself.
  char a[3];
  a[0]='A';
  a[1]='B';
  a[2]='C';

2. **Two dimensional array:** (Oct. 2014, April 2015)
- An array contains more than one index (subscript) is known as two dimensional array.
- Two dimensional array is also known as a matrix.
- A two dimensional array is a grid having rows and columns in which each element is specified by two subscript (See Fig. 4.4).

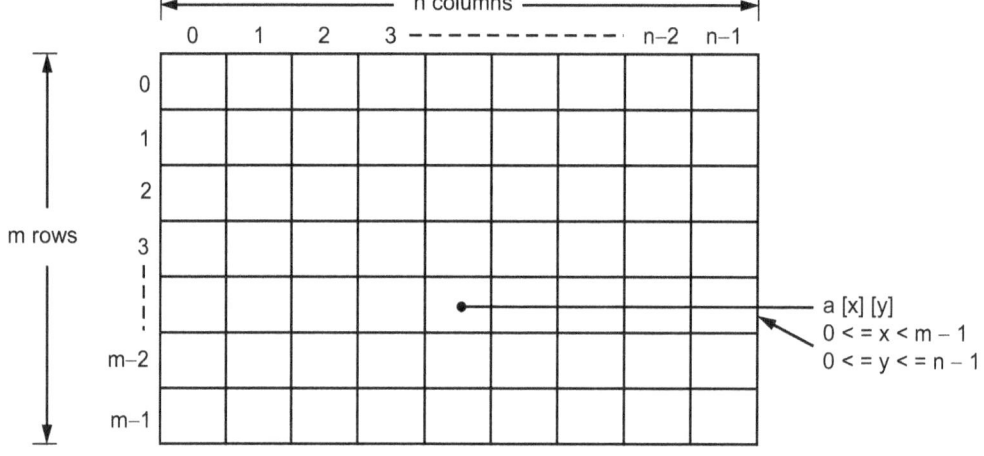

Fig. 4.4

- Fig. 4.5 shows representation of two-dimensional array. In this, we take array [3] [4] containing three rows and four columns and array [0] [2] is an element placed 0th row and 2nd column.

	Column 0	Column 1	Column 2	Column 3	------
Row 0			←		array [0] [2]
Row 1					
Row 2					

Fig. 4.5

3. **Multidimensional Array:**
- Array having more than one subscript variable is called multi-dimensional array.
- Multi-dimensional array is also called as matrix.

4.1.5 Advantages and Disadvantages
Advantages:
1. It is capable of storing many elements at a time.
2. It allows random accessing of elements i.e. any element of the array can be randomly accessed using indexes.
3. You can use one name for similar objects and save them with the same name but with different indices.
4. Arrays are very useful when you are working with sequences of the same kind of data.
5. Arrays use reference type.
6. Not necessity to declare too many variables.
7. Array elements are stored in continuous memory location.

Disadvantages:
1. Predetermining the size of the array is a must.
2. There is a chance of memory wastage or shortage.
3. To delete one element in the array, we need to traverse throughout the array.
4. Sometimes it's not easy to operate with many index arrays.
5. An array uses reference mechanism to work with memory which can cause unstable behaviour of operating system.
6. Wastage of memory space. We cannot change size of array at the run time.
7. It can store only similar type of data.
8. Sometimes it is not easy to operate.

4.2 Maximum and Minimum of Arrays   (Oct. 2014, April 2015)

- The maximum of array is that number which is greater than or equal to all other numbers in the array. This clearly indicates that the maximum may not be unique.
- The minimum of an array is that number which is less than or equal to all other numbers in the array. All numbers in the array need to be examined for finding maximum and minimum of array.
- The simple way to examine every item in an array is to begin with the first element and go on comparing, number by number, until the end of the array is reached. When we begin with the first element, we have no idea of whether or not it is the maximum or minimum. The best thing we can do is write it down as a temporary candidate for the maximum as well as minimum.

Algorithm:
1. Establish an array a[1...n] of n elements where n ≥ 1.
2. Set temporary maximum and temporary minimum to first array element.
3. While less than 'n array elements have been considered do repeatedly
    (a) If next element is greater than or equal to current maximum then assign it to max.
    (b) If next element is less than or equal to current minimum then assign it to min.
4. Return max, min for the array of 'n' elements.

- The number of comparisons required to find the maximum and minimum in an array of 'n' elements is n − 1.

Flowchart for maximum of an array:

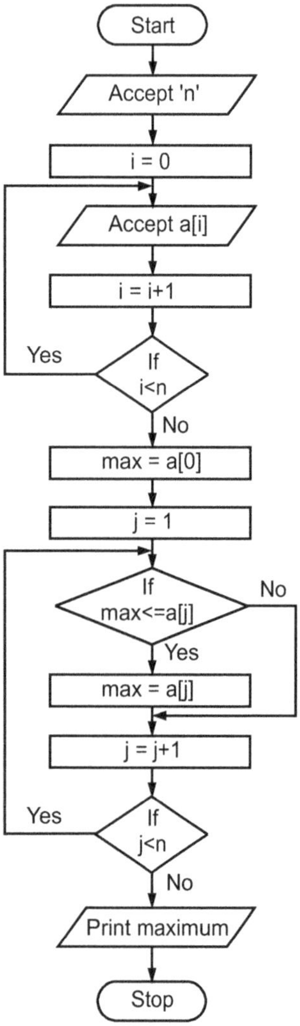

Flowchart for minimum of an array:

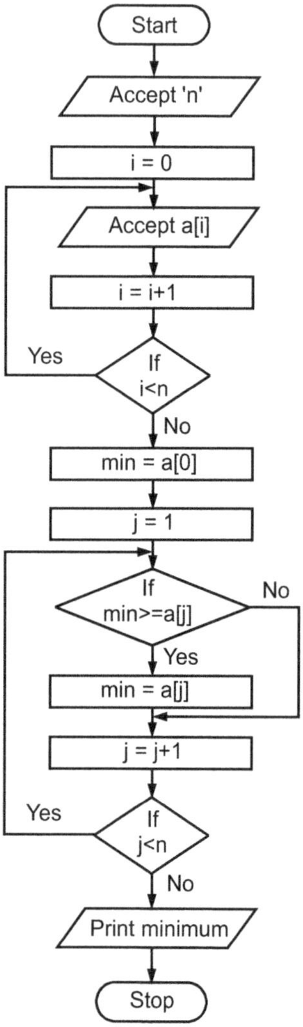

If the algorithm is executed with the following input array, 'a' having 10 elements, then the program execution is as follows.

	0	1	2	3	4	5	6	7	8	9
a	11	12	13	11	15	17	18	20	25	25

Initially, max = min = a[0] = 11.

At first iteration of while loop,

j = 1, i = 10

Since, 11 <= a[1], i.e. 11 <= 12

max = a[1] = 12

The value of min remains unchanged, since

    11 ≯ a[1], i.e. 11 ≯ = 12

i.e. 11 is not greater than or equal to 12.

At second iteration of while loop,

    j = 2, i = 10

Since, 12 <= a[2], i.e. 12 <= 13

    $\boxed{max = a[2] = 13}$

The value of min remains unchanged.

At third iteration of while loop,

    j = 3, i = 10

The value of max remains unchanged because 13 is not less than or equal to 11.

The value of min is just overwritten, because

    11 >= a[3], i.e. 11 >= 11

    $\boxed{min = a[3] = 11}$

At fourth iteration of while loop,

    j = 4, i = 10

Since, 13 <= a[4], i.e. 13 <= 15

    $\boxed{max = a[4] = 15}$

The value of min remains unchanged.

At fifth iteration of while loop,

    j = 5, i = 10

Since, 15 <= a[5], i.e. 15 <= 17

    $\boxed{max = a[5] = 17}$

The value of min remains unchanged.

At sixth iteration of while loop,

    j = 6, i = 10

Since, 17 <= a[6], i.e. 17 <= 18

    $\boxed{max = a[6] = 18}$

The value of min remains unchanged.

At seventh iteration of while loop,

    j = 7, i = 10

Since, 18 <= a[7], i.e. 18 <= 20

    $\boxed{max = a[7] = 20}$

The value of min remains unchanged.

At eighth iteration of while loop,

    j = 8, i = 10

Since, 20 <= a[8], i.e. 20 <= 25

    $\boxed{max = a[8] = 25}$

The value of min remains unchanged.

At ninth iteration of while loop,

    j = 9, i = 10

The value of max is just overwritten, as

    25 <= a[9] i.e. 25 <= 25

    $\boxed{max = a[9] = 25}$

The final values of max and min are 25 and 11 respectively.

The above algorithm can be applied in sorting, scaling applications.

4.2.1 Reversing Elements of an Array

- Our aim here is to rearrange the elements in an array so that they appear in reverse order of the original array.
- For example, an original array before reversal is

	0	1	2	3	4	5	6
a	5	7	4	3	9	6	1

- The array after reversal is

	0	1	2	3	4	5	6
a	1	6	9	3	4	7	5

- The elements exchanged are:
    Iteration 1: a[0] with a[6]
    Iteration 2: a[1] with a[5]
    Iteration 3: a[2] with a[4]
    Iteration 4: a[3] with a[3]   /* no exchange here */
- After, iteration 3 the array is completely reversed. The indices on the left side of the exchanges are in ascending order, while the right side of the exchanges are having descending order.
- The elements are exchanged by using following steps:
    ```
    t = a[i];
    a[i] = a[SIZE - 1 - i];
    a[SIZE - 1 - i] = tmp;
    ```
where, 'SIZE' is the total number of elements in an array.

Algorithm for reversing array elements:
1. Accept the array a[n] having 'n' elements.
2. Find out the number of exchanges needed to reverse the array.
3. While there are pairs of array elements to be exchanged are remaining.
   Exchange the ith element with the [SIZE – 1 – i]th element.
4. Return the reversed array.

Flowchart:

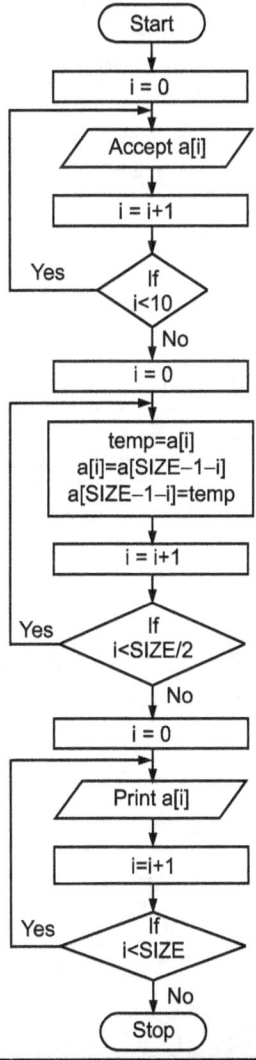

4.3 Mean and Median of n Numbers (April 2015)

- Mean is nothing but the average. For computing mean, we have to add up all the numbers and then divide by the total number of elements.
- To find the median, the numbers have to be listed in numerical order. Here, we have to sort the numbers.

- The median is the 'middle value' in the arranged list.
- When the number of elements in the list are odd, the median is the middle entry in the list after sorting the list in ascending order.
- When the total number of elements in the list are even, the median is equal to the addition of the two middle numbers divided by two. Note that the list must be arranged first before computing the median.
- We can define mean as "adding all the observations and dividing the sum by the number of observations which results the mean.
- We can define median as "the value of the middle item when the data are arranged in an ascending or descending order of magnitude".

Examples:

1. Find the mean and median of 1, 2, 3, 4, 5, 6, 7

$$\text{Mean} = \frac{(1 + 2 + 3 + 4 + 5 + 6 + 7)}{7}$$

$$= \frac{28}{7}$$

$\boxed{\text{Mean} = 4}$

$\boxed{\text{Median} = 4}$ (The middle number)

2. Find mean, and median of 12, 3, 5, 4, 6, 7

$$\text{Mean} = \frac{(12 + 3 + 5 + 4 + 6 + 7)}{6}$$

$$= \frac{37}{6}$$

$\boxed{\text{Mean} = 6.1666}$

For finding median, the numbers are arranged as: 3, 4, 5, 6, 7, 12.
The middle numbers are 5 and 6.

$$\text{Hence, median} = \frac{(5 + 6)}{2}$$

$\boxed{\text{Median} = \frac{11}{2} = 5.5}$

3. Find mean and median of 12, −3, −5, 4, 6, 7

$$\text{Mean} = \frac{(12 - 3 - 5 + 4 + 6 + 7)}{6}$$

$$\text{Mean} = \frac{21}{6} = 3.5$$

For finding median, the numbers are arranged as: −5, −3, 4, 6, 7, 12.

$$\text{Median} = \frac{(4 + 6)}{2}$$

$\boxed{\text{Median} = \frac{10}{2} = 5}$

Algorithm for finding mean of 'n' numbers:

1. Accept an array having fixed number of elements.
2. Set index variable and variable for storing the sum to zero.
3. While index variable is less than the total number of elements in array do repeatedly
   (a) Add the elements of array into the sum variable.
   (b) Increment index variable by one. (i.e. the value of index variable).
4. Divide the total sum by the total number of elements.
5. Return the result obtained in Step 4.

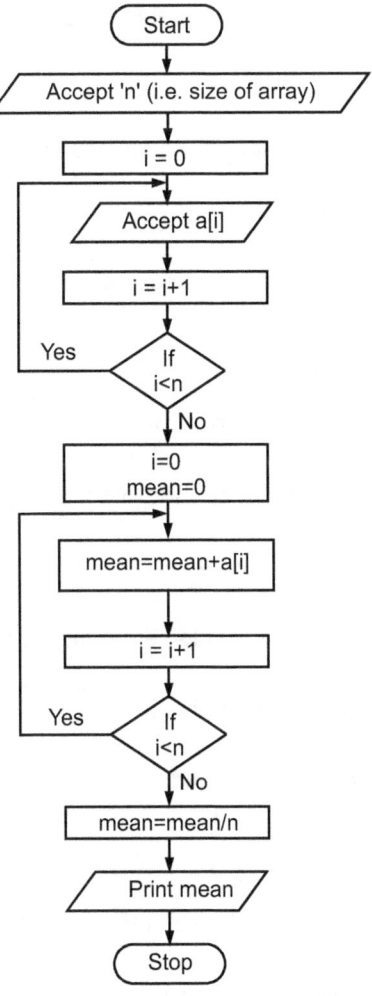

Algorithm for finding median of 'n' numbers:

1. Accept an array having fixed (finite) number of elements.

2. Set the value of first index variable 'i' to zero. Also set temporary variable's value to zero.

3. While first index variable's value less than the total number of elements (i.e. size) of array do repeatedly

    (a) Set second index variable to zero.

    (b) While second index variable's value is one less than the size of array do repeatedly

    (i) If the value of current array index position is less than or equal to the next array index position then

      Interchange the values at these positions.

    else

    Skip to the next iteration of the loop.

    (ii) Increment value of second index variable by 1.

    (c) Increment value of first index variable by 1.

4. If size of array (i.e. total number of elements) mod 2 equals to zero then

    (i.e. there are even number of elements in array)

    return the average of the two middle elements in the array

    else

    (i.e. there are odd number of elements in array)

    return the value at the middle position in the array.

Flowchart:

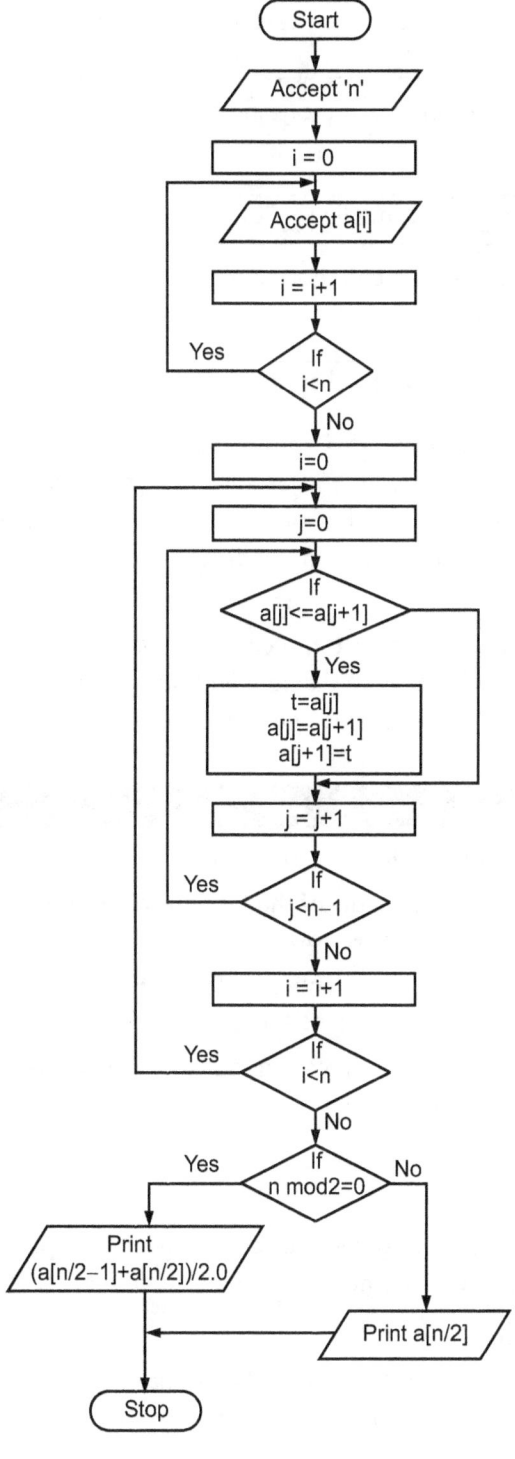

Usage of mean and median in practice:

- Mean is considered as an economic measure whereas median is considered as a social measure.

   Example 1: The values given are in thousands.

   30, 40, 50, 60, 70.

   In this case, $\boxed{\text{mean} = 50}$ and $\boxed{\text{median} = 50}$.

   Example 2: The values given are in thousands.

   30, 40, 50, 60, 700.

   In this case, $\boxed{\text{mean} = 176}$ and $\boxed{\text{median} = 50}$

- If the above data belongs to salary information of employees, then the mean is affected by the extreme (outlier) value 700, in example 2. On the other hand, median remains unaffected. The mean income of a group of persons might be of more interest to retailers and also the tax office. But median income might be of more interest to employee welfare organisations.

- In construction and real estate sector, a customer wanting to buy a flat (or home) from the builder would use the median (i.e. middle house value). This is due to the fact that there are extremely high cost values in the data set, which can affect the mean value of the flat (or home).

4.4 Array Representation

- Arrays may be represented in Row-major form or Column-major form.
- In Row-major form, all the elements of the first row are printed, then the elements of the second row and so on upto the last row.
- In Column-major form, all the elements of the first column are printed, then the elements of the second column and so on upto the last column.
- A 2D array's elements are stored in continuous memory locations. It can be represented in memory using any of the following two ways:
   1. Column-major order, and
   2. Row-major order
- A 2-dimensional array is having two indices, of which first specifies the number of rows and the second specifies the number of columns of an array.

   For example, int A[3][4];

- The above declaration tells us that A is 2-D array having 3 rows and 4 columns. The row and column arrangement of 2-D array forms a matrix like structure.

For example, int A[3] [4] = {{19, 20, 31, 41},
{50, 51, 71, 89},
{90, 91, 95, 99}
};

- The array 'A' is represented as follows:

Columns

Rows	0	1	2	3
0	19	20	31	41
1	50	51	71	89
2	90	91	95	99

- Actually, the above matrix elements are stored linearly, since memory of computer can only be viewed as sequential units of memory. There are two possible arrangements of elements in memory, namely Row-major order and Column-major order.
- Row-major order is employed by high-level-programming languages like Pascal, C, Ada etc. Column-major order is used in FORTRAN and various dialects of BASIC.

4.4.1 Row-major Form of Array Representation (Oct. 2014)

- In Row-major form, all the elements of the first row are printed, then the elements of the second row and so on upto the last row.
- A two dimensional array, where the elements are stored row by row is said to have row major order of the array.
- In this method the elements are stored row wise, i.e. n elements of first row are stored in first n locations, n elements of second row are stored in next n locations and so on. For example, A 3 × 4 array will be stored as below.

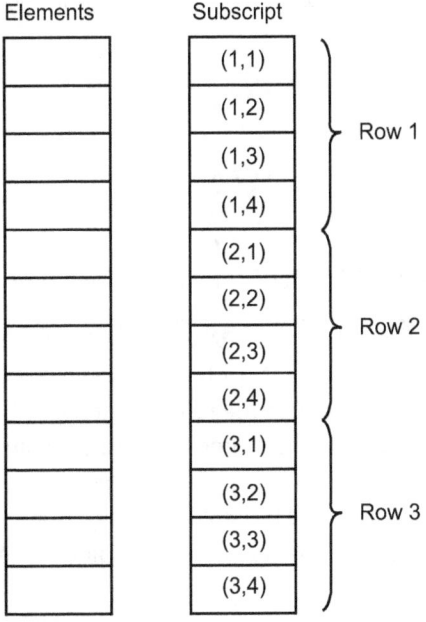

- For example, the previous array A[3][4] would be stored in memory in Row-major order with the array cells continuously stored as shown below.

100	102	104	106	108	110	112	114	116	118	120	122
19	20	31	41	50	51	71	89	90	91	95	99

|← Row '0' →|← Row '1' →|← Row '2' →|

- The numbers written above the array cells ranging from 100 to 122 shows the memory offset. Here by definition each integer takes two bytes. Hence, the difference between two adjacent offsets is two.
- The linear offset from the beginning of the array to any specific element A[row][column] can be found as:

    offset=(row*n+column)*2

    where, 'n' is the number of columns in the array.
- 'C' language labels the first element of array index by zero. Row 1, Column 2 in matrix A is represented by A[0][1].

    1. The offset for A[0][1] is computed as follows.

    $$\text{Offset} = (0 * 4 + 1) * 2$$
    $$= 1 * 2$$
    $$= 2$$

- Hence, elements 20 (i.e. A[0][1] is at 102, which is nothing but base address + offset (i.e. 100 + 2).

    2. The offset for A[2][3]

    $$= (2 * 4 + 3) * 2$$
    $$= 11 * 2$$
    $$= 22$$

    Element 99 (i.e. A[2][3] is at 122 which is equal to base address + offset (i.e. 100 + 22)).

4.4.2 Column-major Form of Array Representation   (April 2015)

- In column-major form, all the elements of the first column are printed, then the elements of the second column and so on upto the last column.
- The two dimensional array which is stored column by column is said to have column major order on the array.
- In this method the elements are stored column wise, i.e. m elements of first column are stored in first m locations, m elements of second column are stored in next m locations and so on.

- For example, A 3 × 4 array will be stored as below.

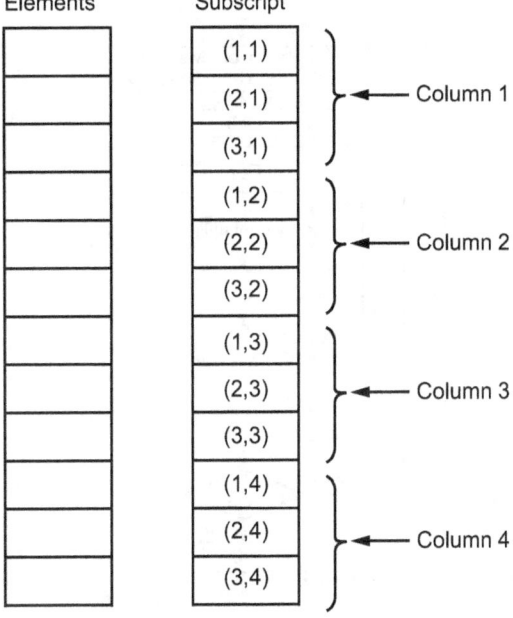

- For example, the array A[3][4] would be stored in memory in column-major order with the array cells contiguously stored as shown below.

100	102	104	106	108	110	112	114	116	118	120	122
19	50	90	20	51	91	31	71	95	41	89	99

|←— Column '0' —→|←— Column '1' —→|←— Column '2' —→|←— Column '3' —→|

- The numbers written above in array cells shows the memory offset. The difference between two adjacent offsets is two.
- The linear offset from the beginning of the array to any specific element A[row] [column] can be found as:

$$\text{offset} = (\text{row} + \text{column} * n) * 2$$

where, 'n' is the number of rows in the array.

1. The offset for A[2][1] (i.e. 91) is computed as follows:

$$\text{offset} = (2 + 1 * 3) * 2$$
$$\text{offset} = 5 * 2 = 10$$

The element 91 (i.e. A[2][1] is at 110, which is nothing but base address + offset (i.e. 100 + 10)).

2. The offset for A[2][2] (i.e. 95) is computed as follows:

$$\text{offset} = (2 + 2 * 3) * 2$$
$$\text{offset} = 8 * 2 = 16$$

- The element 95 (i.e. A[2][2] is at 116, which is nothing but base address + offset (i.e. 100 + 16). The program for printing row-major and column-major representation of a matrix array is as follows.

Flowchart:

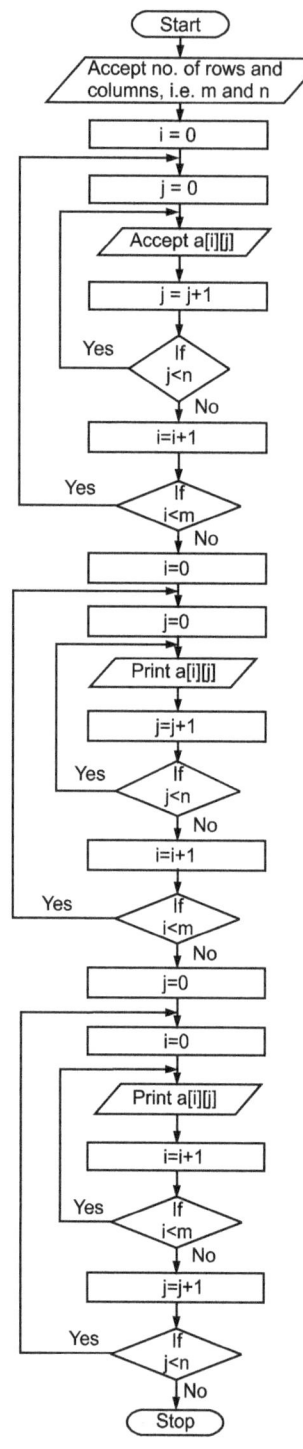

Algorithm:
1. Accept an array having 'm' rows and 'n' columns.
2. Initialize 'i' to zero.
3. While 'i' is less than the number of row (i.e. 'm')
   do repeatedly
   (a) Initialize 'j' to zero.
   (b) While 'j' is less than the number of columns (i.e. 'n') do repeatedly
       (i) Print a[i][j] element (i.e. i^{th} row, j^{th} column)
       (ii) Increment 'j' by 1.
   (c) Increment 'i' by 1.
4. Initialize 'j' to zero.
5. While 'j' is less than the number of columns (i.e. 'n') do repeatedly
   (a) Initialize 'i' to zero.
   (b) While 'i' is less than the number of rows (i.e. 'm') do repeatedly
       (i) Print a[i][j] element (i.e. i^{th} row, j^{th} column)
       (ii) Increment 'i' by 1.
   (c) Increment 'j' by 1.

4.5 Matrices
- A matrix is an arrangement of numbers in row and column format.
- For example,

$$L = \begin{bmatrix} 1 & 2 & 3 \\ 6 & 4 & 8 \\ 7 & 9 & 5 \end{bmatrix}$$

- Here L denotes the matrix and has three rows and three columns. It is a 3 × 3 matrix.

4.5.1 Addition (Oct. 2014)
- To add two matrices, they should be of the same size. That means two matrices must be of same dimensions.
- For example:

1. $A = \begin{bmatrix} 0 & 1 & 2 \\ 3 & 4 & 5 \end{bmatrix}, B = \begin{bmatrix} 4 & 6 & 8 \\ 2 & 5 & 9 \end{bmatrix}$

'A' is a 2 × 3 matrix, 'B' is also a 2 × 3 matrix. Hence, their addition is possible.

$$A + B = \begin{bmatrix} 0+4 & 1+6 & 2+8 \\ 3+2 & 4+5 & 5+9 \end{bmatrix}$$

$$A + B = \begin{bmatrix} 4 & 7 & 10 \\ 5 & 9 & 14 \end{bmatrix}$$

The addition of two matrices A + B is again 2 × 3 matrix.

2. $A = \begin{bmatrix} 1 & 2 \\ 3 & 4 \end{bmatrix}, B = \begin{bmatrix} 5 & 6 & 7 \\ 8 & 5 & 9 \end{bmatrix}$

'A' is a 2 × 2 matrix, 'B' is a 2 × 3 matrix. Hence, their addition is not possible.

Algorithm for addition of two matrices is given below:

1. Accept the total number of rows, i.e. 'm'.
2. Accept the total number of columns, i.e. 'n'.
3. Set 'i' to zero.
4. While 'i' is less than 'm' do repeatedly
    (a) Set j to zero.
    (b) While j is less than 'n' do repeatedly
        (i) Accept value for i^{th} row, j^{th} column for first array i.e. a[i][j].
        (ii) Increment value of j by 1.
    (c) Increment value of i by 1.
5. Set 'i' to zero.
6. While 'i' is less than 'm' do repeatedly
    (a) Set j to zero.
    (b) While 'j' is less than 'n' do repeatedly
        (i) Accept value for i^{th} row, j^{th} column for second array, i.e. b[i][j].
        (ii) Increment value of j by 1.
    (c) Increment value of i by 1.
7. Set 'i' to zero.
8. While 'i' is less than 'm' do repeatedly
    (a) Set j to zero.
    (b) While 'j' is less than 'n' do repeatedly
        (i) Add a[i][j] into b[i][j].
        (ii) Print the addition.
        (iii) Increment value of 'j' by 1.
    (c) Increment value of 'i' by 1.

Steps 4 and 6 accept two matrices A and B respectively.

Flowchart:

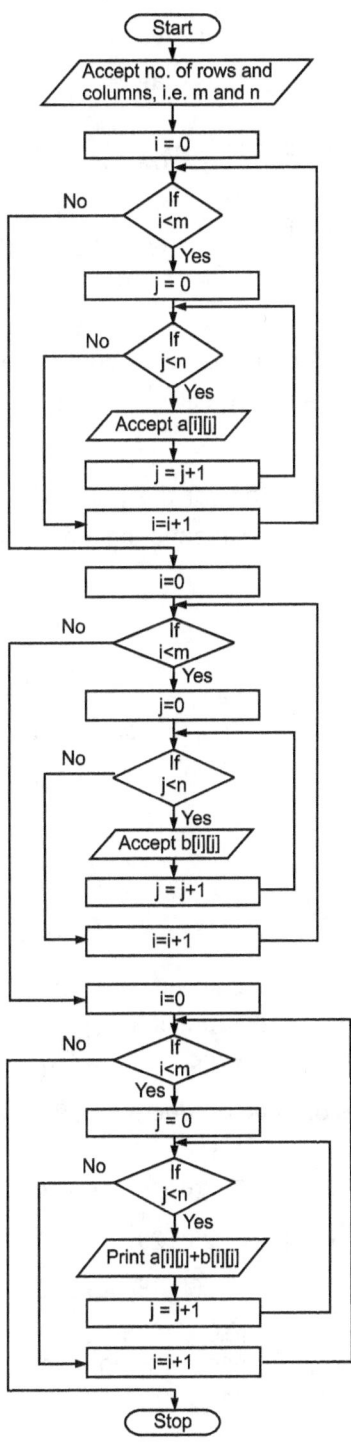

- The addition of two matrices 'A' and 'B' is written in notational format as:

$$A = \begin{bmatrix} a_{11} & a_{12} \\ a_{21} & a_{22} \end{bmatrix} \quad B = \begin{bmatrix} b_{11} & b_{12} \\ b_{21} & b_{22} \end{bmatrix}$$

$$A + B = \begin{bmatrix} a_{11} + b_{11} & a_{12} + b_{12} \\ a_{21} + b_{21} & a_{22} + b_{22} \end{bmatrix}$$

$$A + B = \begin{bmatrix} b_{11} + a_{11} & b_{12} + a_{12} \\ b_{21} + a_{21} & b_{22} + a_{22} \end{bmatrix}$$

$$\therefore \boxed{A + B = B + A}$$

- The above assumes that both matrices have same dimensions (same number of rows and columns). The practical application of matrix addition is explained through the following example.

Example 1: The sale of four quarters for the year 2010 and 2011 of ball pen, fountain pen and pencils are given below. (Figures mentioned are in thousands).

Year 2010

$$A = \begin{matrix} \text{Ball pen} \\ \text{Fountain Pen} \\ \text{Pencil} \end{matrix} \begin{bmatrix} Q1 & Q2 & Q3 & Q4 \\ 10 & 20 & 15 & 20 \\ 20 & 20 & 15 & 20 \\ 30 & 25 & 15 & 20 \end{bmatrix}$$

Year 2011

$$B = \begin{matrix} \text{Ball pen} \\ \text{Fountain Pen} \\ \text{Pencil} \end{matrix} \begin{bmatrix} Q1 & Q2 & Q3 & Q4 \\ 10 & 5 & 15 & 20 \\ 15 & 20 & 25 & 10 \\ 10 & 15 & 20 & 5 \end{bmatrix}$$

Find out total quarterly sales of three products, for 2010 and 2011.

Solution:

$$A + B = \begin{bmatrix} 10 & 20 & 15 & 20 \\ 20 & 20 & 15 & 20 \\ 30 & 25 & 15 & 20 \end{bmatrix} + \begin{bmatrix} 10 & 5 & 15 & 20 \\ 15 & 20 & 25 & 10 \\ 10 & 15 & 20 & 5 \end{bmatrix}$$

$$A + B = \begin{bmatrix} 10+10 & 20+5 & 15+15 & 20+20 \\ 20+15 & 20+20 & 15+25 & 20+10 \\ 30+10 & 25+15 & 15+20 & 20+5 \end{bmatrix}$$

$$A + B = \begin{bmatrix} 20 & 25 & 30 & 40 \\ 35 & 40 & 40 & 30 \\ 40 & 40 & 35 & 25 \end{bmatrix}$$

4.5.2 Matrix Multiplication

- Two matrices can be multiplied only if the number of columns of the first matrix equals the number of rows of the second matrix.

- The matrix resulting from the multiplication will have the number of rows equal to the first matrix and number of columns equal to the second matrix.

- That means, a matrix of the order m × n can only be multiplied with a matrix of order n × p. The resultant matrix will have the order m × p.

- The multiplication of two matrices 'A' and 'B' is computed as follows.

$$A = \begin{bmatrix} a_{11} & a_{12} \\ a_{21} & a_{22} \end{bmatrix} \quad B = \begin{bmatrix} b_{11} & b_{12} & b_{13} \\ b_{21} & b_{22} & b_{23} \end{bmatrix}$$

$$A \times B = \begin{bmatrix} (a_{11} * b_{11}) + (a_{12} * b_{21}) & (a_{11} * b_{12}) + (a_{12} * b_{22}) & (a_{11} * b_{13}) + (a_{12} * b_{23}) \\ (a_{21} * b_{11}) + (a_{22} * b_{21}) & (a_{21} * b_{12}) + (a_{22} * b_{22}) & (a_{21} * b_{13}) + (a_{22} * b_{23}) \end{bmatrix}$$

A is 2 × 2 matrix, B is 2 × 3 matrix.

A × B is 2 × 3 matrix.

Algorithm for matrix multiplication:

1. Accept first matrix 'A' having 'm' rows and 'n' columns (i.e. m * n values).

2. Accept the values of rows and columns for second matrix (i.e. 'X' rows and 'Y' columns).

3. If the number of columns of the first matrix (i.e. 'n') not equal to the number of rows of the second matrix (i.e. 'X') then

   (a) Print message.

   (b) Terminate the process.

   Else

   (a) Accept second matrix having 'X' rows and 'Y' columns (i.e. x * y values).

(b) Set the value of i to zero.

(c) While i less than the number of rows of the first matrix (i.e. i < m) do repeatedly

    (i)   Set value of j to zero.

        C.1 While j is less than the number of columns of the second matrix (i.e. j < y) do repeatedly

            C.1 (i)   Set value of k to zero.

                C.1.1 While k less than the number of rows of the second matrix (i.e. k < x) do repeatedly

                      C.1.1. (i)   Compute latest sum by adding the multiplication of a[i][k] * b[k][j] to the previous sum.

                      C.1.1 (ii)   Increment k by 1.

            C.1 (ii)   Assign latest sum to C[i][j] (i.e. the ith row, j^{th} column of resultant matrix).

            C.1 (iii)   Set sum to zero.

            C.1 (iv)   Increment value of j by 1.

    (ii)   Increment value of i by 1.

(d) Set value of i to zero.

(e) While i less than the number of rows of first matrix (i.e. m) do repeatedly

    (i)   Set value of j to zero.

    e.1   While j less than the number of columns of second matrix (i.e. y) do repeatedly

        e.1 (i)   Print C[i][j]

        e.1 (ii)   Increment value of j by 1.

    (ii)   Increment value of i by 1.

Flowchart:

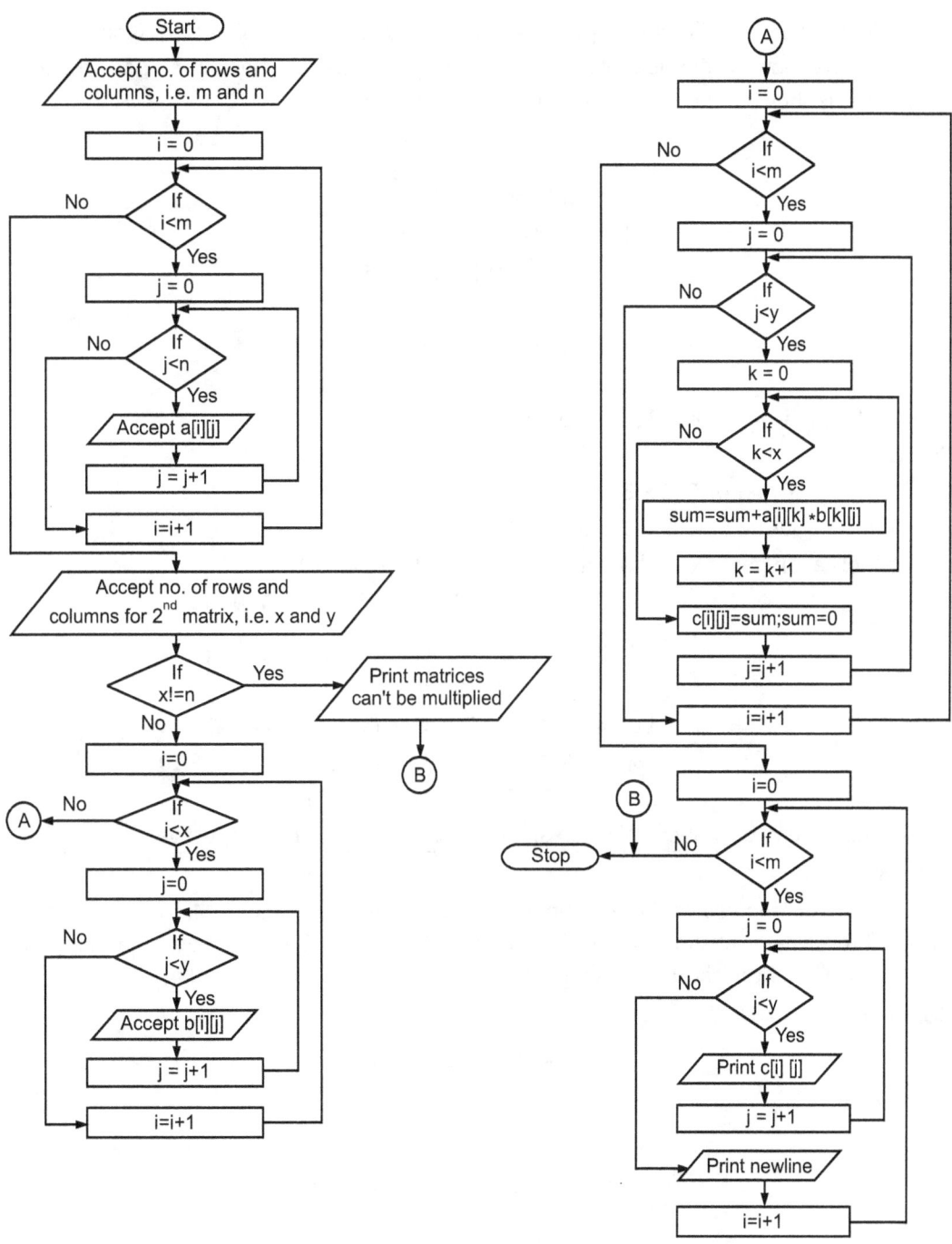

The practical application of matrix multiplication is explained below.

Example 1:

Mahesh, Yogesh and Chinmay purchased ball pens of different brands, A, B and C. Let T be the matrix showing the quantity of each brand purchased by these three persons. Let C be the matrix showing the price of each brand of ball pen.

$$T = \begin{array}{c} \\ \text{Mahesh} \\ \text{Yogesh} \\ \text{Chinmay} \end{array} \begin{array}{ccc} A & B & C \\ \begin{bmatrix} 5 & 7 & 3 \\ 6 & 4 & 2 \\ 10 & 8 & 9 \end{bmatrix} \end{array}$$

$$C = \begin{array}{c} A \\ B \\ C \end{array} \begin{bmatrix} 5 \\ 10 \\ 5 \end{bmatrix}$$

Find the total amount of ₹ spend by these three:

Solution:

Order of T : 3 × **3** (i.e. m × n)

Order of C : **3** × 1 (i.e. n × q)

Multiplication possible and order of T × C is 3 × 1 (i.e. m × q)

$$T \times C = \begin{bmatrix} 5 & 7 & 3 \\ 6 & 4 & 2 \\ 10 & 8 & 9 \end{bmatrix} \times \begin{bmatrix} 5 \\ 10 \\ 5 \end{bmatrix} = \begin{bmatrix} 110 \\ 80 \\ 175 \end{bmatrix}$$

110 = (5 * 5) + (7 * 10) + (3 * 5) = 25 + 70 + 15

80 = (6 * 5) + (4 * 10) + (2 * 5) + 30 + 40 + 10

175 = (10 * 5) + (8 * 10) + (9 * 5) = 50 + 80 + 45

Amount spend by Mahesh, Yogesh and Chinmay is 110, 80, 175 respectively.

Example 2:

Let matrix Q represents the quantity purchased in kilos by Mandar. Matrix 'T' represents prices of these items at shop 'A' (which is adjacent to his home) and at shop 'B'. Assume that cost of travelling from shop 'A' to shop 'B' is 30. Find total savings of Mandar.

Solution:

Given:

$$Q = \begin{array}{ccc} \text{Rice} & \text{Sugar} & \text{Wheat} \\ [5 & 10 & 5] \end{array}$$

$$T = \begin{array}{c} \\ \text{Rice} \\ \text{Sugar} \\ \text{Wheat} \end{array} \begin{array}{cc} \text{Shop 'A'} & \text{Shop 'B'} \\ \begin{bmatrix} 20 & 15 \\ 10 & 7 \\ 7 & 5 \end{bmatrix} \end{array}$$

$$\text{Total price} = Q \times T = \begin{bmatrix} 5 & 10 & 5 \end{bmatrix} \times \begin{bmatrix} 20 & 15 \\ 10 & 7 \\ 7 & 5 \end{bmatrix}$$

$$= \begin{bmatrix} 235 & 170 \end{bmatrix}$$

Cost of purchasing from shop 'A' = 235.

Cost of purchasing from shop 'B' = 170 + 30 = 200.

∴ Total savings to Mandar, if purchasing made from shop 'B' = 235 − 200 = 35.

4.5.3 Transpose of Matrix

- Transpose of a matrix of an array is obtained by interchanging the rows and columns of a square matrix.
- The transpose of a matrix 'A' is denoted by A^T. A^T has 'n' rows and 'm' columns. The rows of A are columns of A^T and the columns of A are rows of A^T. Transpose of A^T is nothing but A again.

i.e. $(A^T)^T = A$

Example:

$$A = \begin{bmatrix} 5 & -1 \\ 15 & 9 \end{bmatrix}$$

$$A^T = \begin{bmatrix} 5 & 15 \\ -1 & 9 \end{bmatrix}$$

Algorithm:

Step 1: Accept the values of row and column (i.e. total number of rows 'm' and total number of columns 'n').

Step 2: Set i to zero.

Step 3: While 'i' less than 'm' do repeatedly
    (a) Set j to zero.
    (b) While 'j' less than 'n' do repeatedly
        (i) Accept value for a[i][j].
        (ii) Increment value of j by 1.
    (c) Increment value of i by 1.

Step 4: Set i to zero.
    /* Rows and columns values are exchanged */

Step 5: While i less than 'n' do repeatedly
    (a) Set j to zero.
    (b) While 'j' less than 'm' do repeatedly
        (i) Print value for a[j][i]
        (ii) Increment value of j by 1.
    (c) Increment value of 'i' by 1.

Flowchart:

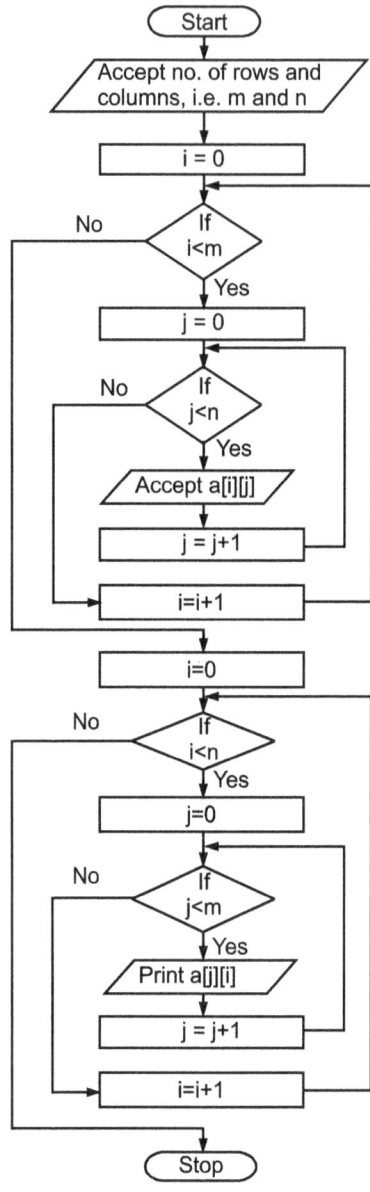

If A and B are matrices of the same size, then,

$$(A + B)^T = A^T + B^T$$

4.5.4 Matrix Symmetry

- A symmetric matrix is a square matrix, for which $a_{ij} = a_{ji}$, is symmetric about its main diagonal (i.e. top left to bottom right).

- In other words "a symmetric matrix is a square matrix that is equal to its transpose" and "the elements of a symmetric matrix are symmetric with respect to the main diagonal".
- The following are symmetric matrices.

$$A = \begin{bmatrix} 1 & 2 \\ 2 & 4 \end{bmatrix} \quad B = \begin{bmatrix} 1 & 2 & 6 \\ 2 & 3 & 4 \\ 6 & 4 & 5 \end{bmatrix}$$

- The main diagonal acts as a mirror line.
- A antisymmetric or skew-symmetric matrix is a square matrix, for which $a_{ij} = -a_{ji}$. The main diagonal entries of the antisymmetric or skew-symmetric matrix must be zero.
- The following is an antisymmetric matrix of order 3.

$$C = \begin{bmatrix} 0 & 2 & -1 \\ -2 & 0 & 5 \\ 1 & -5 & 0 \end{bmatrix}$$

The algorithm for checking matrix symmetry is as follows:
1. Initialise flag to zero.
2. Accept the values for total number of rows (i.e. m) and total number of columns (i.e. n).
3. Set i to zero.
4. While 'i' less than 'm' do repeatedly
   (a) Set j to zero.
   (b) While 'j' less than 'n' do repeatedly
       (i) Accept value for a[i][j].
       (ii) Increment value of j by 1.
   (c) Increment value of i by 1.
5. Set i to zero.
6. While 'i' less than 'm' do repeatedly
   (a) Set j to zero.
   (b) While j less than 'n' do repeatedly
       (i) Assign to b[i][j] the value of a[j][i] by interchanging row and column positions.
       (ii) Increment value of 'j' by 1.
   (c) Increment value of i by 1.
7. Set i to zero.
8. While 'i' less than 'm' do repeatedly
   (a) Set j to zero.
   (b) While 'j' less than 'n' do repeatedly
       (i) If the element at i^{th} row, j^{th} column of matrix B does not match with the same positions of matrix A then
           Set flag to 1.
       (ii) Increment value of 'j' by 1.
   (c) Increment value of 'i' by 1.

9. If flag equals to 1 then
   print message "Not symmetric"
   else
   print message "Symmetric"

Flowchart:

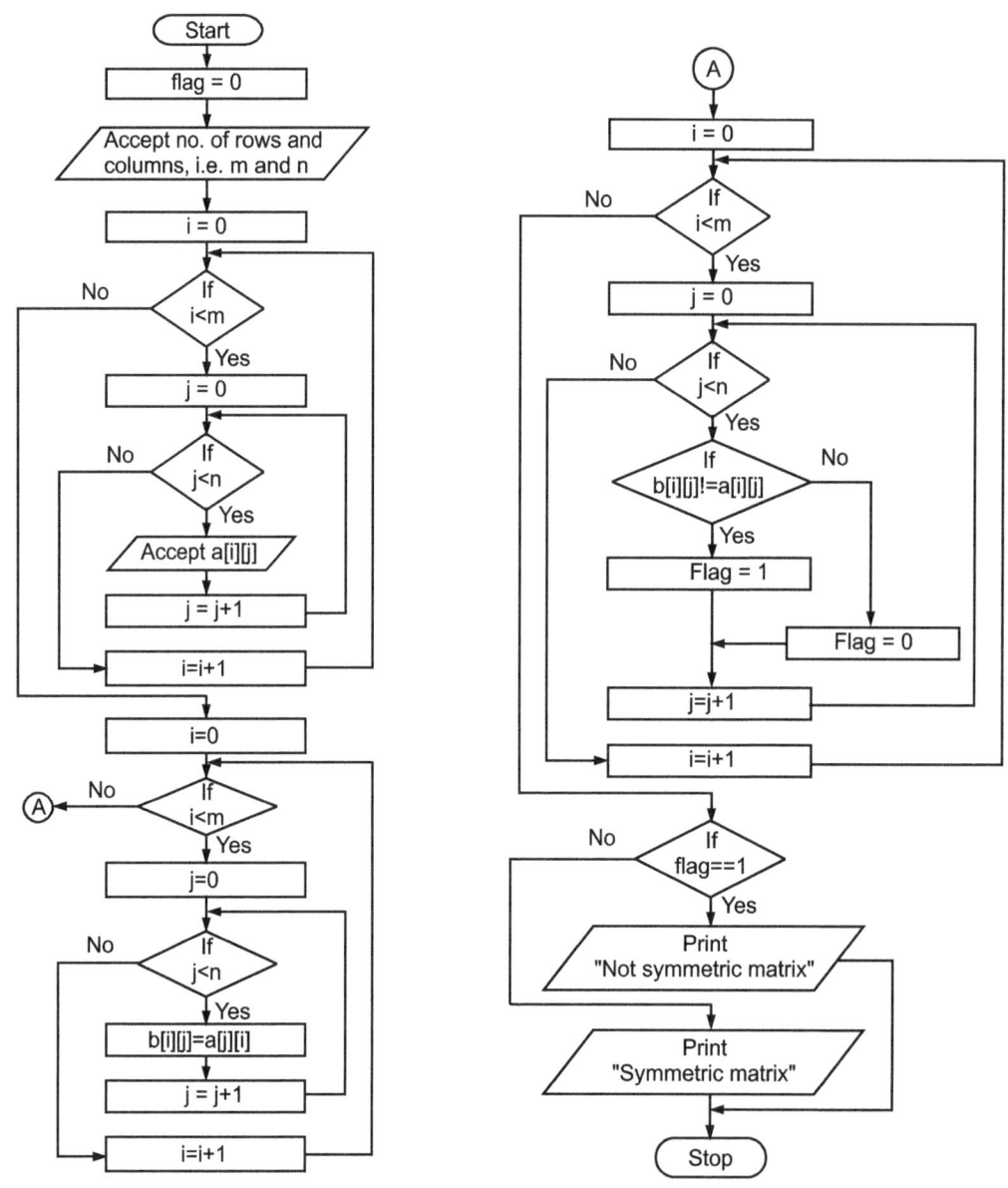

Note: If A is any symmetric matrix, then the matrix is equal to its transpose.
i.e. $A = A^T$.

4.5.5 Upper and Lower Triangular Matrix (April 2015)

- A matrix that is both upper and lower triangular is a diagonal matrix.

1. Lower triangular matrix:

- A square matrix is called lower triangular if all the entries above the main diagonal (i.e. from top left to bottom right) are zero.

  i.e. $a_{ij} = 0$, where $i < j$.

  Example 1: $A = \begin{bmatrix} 1 & 0 & 0 \\ 2 & 4 & 0 \\ 3 & 5 & 6 \end{bmatrix}$ is lower triangular matrix.

  Here, $a_{12} = 0$ (Since, $1 < 2$)

  $a_{13} = 0$ (Since $1 < 3$)

  $a_{23} = 0$ (Since, $2 < 3$)

2. Upper triangular matrix:

- A square matrix is called upper triangular if all the entries below the main diagonal (i.e. from top left to bottom right) are zero.

  i.e. $a_{ij} = 0$, where $i > j$.

  Example 2: $B = \begin{bmatrix} 1 & 4 & 3 \\ 0 & 5 & 7 \\ 0 & 0 & 2 \end{bmatrix}$ is upper triangular matrix.

  Here, $b_{21} = 0$ (Since, $2 > 1$)

  $b_{31} = 0$ (Since, $3 > 1$)

  $b_{32} = 0$ (Since, $3 > 2$)

> **Note:** Diagonal matrices are both upper and lower triangular, since they have zeros above and below the main diagonal.
>
> **Example:** $C = \begin{bmatrix} 1 & 0 & 0 \\ 0 & 2 & 0 \\ 0 & 0 & 3 \end{bmatrix}$ is a diagonal matrix.

Here, C is both upper and lower triangular.

Algorithm:

1. Accept the number of rows and number of columns (i.e. m and n).
2. If number of rows equal to the number of columns (i.e. m = n) then

/* which is a square matrix */
(a) Set value of i to zero.
(b) While 'i' less than 'm' do repeatedly
    b.1 Set j to zero.
    b.2 While j less than 'n' do repeatedly
        (i) Accept value for a[i][j].
        (ii) Increment value of j by 1.
    b.3 Increment value of i by 1.
/* Logic for lower triangular matrix */
(c) Set value of i to zero.
(d) While 'i' less than 'm' do repeatedly
    d.1 Set j to zero.
    d.2 While 'j' less than 'n' do repeatedly
        d.2.1 If row position $\geq$ column position then
            print value of a[i][j]
            else
            print zero.
        d.2.2 Increment value of j by 1.
    d.3 Increment value of i by 1.
/* Logic for upper triangular matrix */
(e) Set value of i to zero.
(f) While 'i' less than 'm' do repeatedly
    f.1 Set j to zero.
    f.2 While 'j' less than 'n' do repeatedly
        f.2.1 If row position $\leq$ column position then
            print value of a[i][j]
            else
            print zero.
        f.2.2 Increment value of j by 1.
    f.3 Increment value of 'i' by 1.
/* 'else' of 'if' mentioned at step 2, indicating the matrix is a non-square matrix */
    else
/* for non-square matrix algorithm stops */
print message

Flowchart:

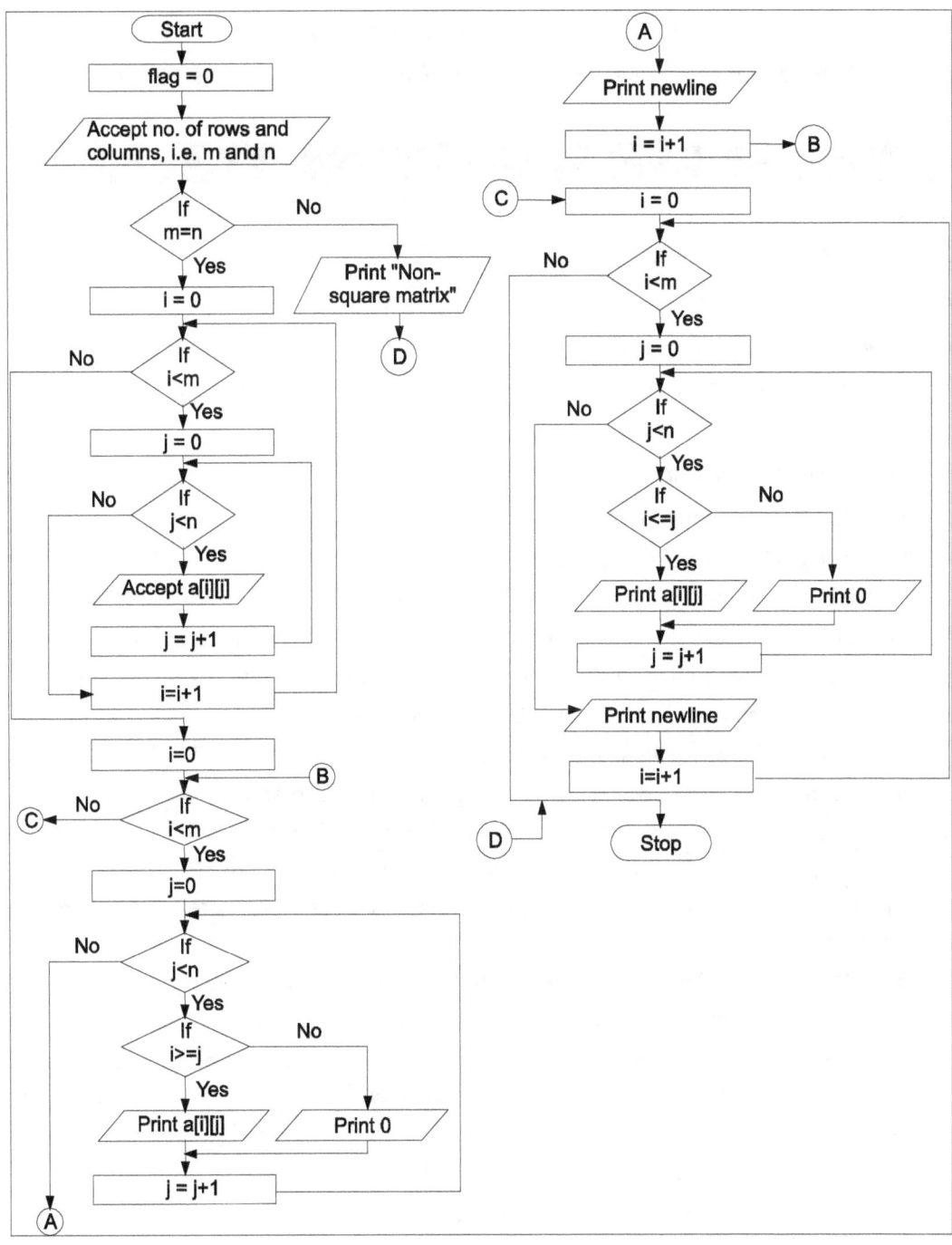

Matrices are used in various applications like:

(i) **Graph Theory:** Adjacency matrix of a graph.

(ii) **Computer Graphics:** Transformation, rotation matrices

(iii) **Cryptography:** Encoding, decoding and sending secret messages using matrices.

Questions

1. What is an array?
2. Explain the characteristics of array in detail.
3. How to define array?
4. What are the types of arrays?
5. Define the following terms:
   (i) Array
   (ii) One dimensional array
   (iii) Multidimensional array
6. What is median and mean and array?
7. Write short notes on maximum and minimum of array.
8. Explain the row-major and column-major forms of array representation.
9. Write an algorithm to find the maximum and minimum of an array having 'n' elements.
10. Discuss any one example which involves matrix multiplication.
11. Write an algorithm to reverse the elements of an array.
12. What is the difference between lower and upper triangular matrix?
13. State the difference between steps while calculating mean and median.
14. If the base address is 200 and the difference between two adjacent offsets is 2, calculate the offset for a[2][3] in row-major representation. Assume that, there are 4 columns in an array.
15. State the difference between symmetric and skew-symmetric matrix with example.
16. State the conditions to check before addition of two matrices.
17. If the base address is 500 and the difference between two adjacent offsets is 2, calculate the offset for a[3][4] in column-major representation. Assume that, there are 3 rows in an array.
18. What is 2-D array? Explain in brief.
19. List the applications in which matrices are used.
20. Draw a flowchart for matrix transpose.

University Questions and Answers

October 2014

1. Explain 2-Dimesional Array in brief. **[2M]**

   Ans. Please refer to Section 4.1.4, Point (2).

2. What is Row major of matrix? **[2M]**

   Ans. Please refer to Section 4.4.1.

3. Write an algorithm to find maximum of an array. **[4M]**

   Ans. Please refer to Section 4.2.

4. Write a short note on an array. **[4M]**

   Ans. Please refer to Section 4.1.

5. Write an algorithm for addition of 2 matrices. **[4M]**

   Ans. Please refer to Section 4.5.1.

April 2015

1. What is an Array? **[2 M]**

   Ans. Please refer to Sections 4.1 and 4.1.1.

2. Explain column majors of matrix. **[2 M]**

   Ans. Please refer to Section 4.4.2.

3. Explain 2-Dimesional Array in brief. **[2 M]**

   Ans. Please refer to Section 4.1.4 Point (2).

4. What is mean? [2 M]

Ans. Please refer to Section 4.3.

5. Write an algorithm to find minimum of an array. [4 M]

Ans. Please refer to Section 4.2.

6. Explain types of arrays with examples. [4 M]

Ans. Please refer to Section 4.1.4.

7. Explain the term upper and lower triangle matrix. [4 M]

Ans. Please refer to Section 4.5.5.

Chapter 5...

Sorting and Searching

Contents ...

5.1 Introduction

5.2 Sorting

    5.2.1 Definition

    5.2.2 Sorting Algorithms

    5.2.3 Classification Criteria for Sorting Algorithms

5.3 Sorting Techniques

    5.3.1 Bubble Sort

    5.3.2 Selection Sort

    5.3.3 Insertion Sort

    5.3.4 Merge Sort

    5.3.5 Radix Sort

    5.3.6 Shell Sort

    5.3.7 Quick Sort

    5.3.8 Counting Sort

    5.3.9 Bucket Sort

5.4 Searching

    5.4.1 Linear Search

        5.4.1.1 Definition

        5.4.1.2 Advantages and Disadvantages

    5.4.2 Binary Search

        5.4.2.1 Definition

        5.4.2.2 Advantages and Disadvantages

- Questions
- University Questions and Answers

5.1 Introduction

- Arranging the data in either ascending or descending manner based on certain key in the record is known as sorting.
- The process of finding a particular record is known as searching.
- An algorithm that puts elements of a list in a certain order is known as a sorting algorithm.
- An algorithm for finding an item with specified properties among a collection of items or elements is known as search algorithm.

5.2 Sorting

- Sorting is a method of arranging or ordering records of element of a table in a logical order (alphabetically), in a numeric order (ascending/descending).
- In order words "sorting is an operation that segregates items or elements into groups according to specified criteration".
- The sorting is classified into two categories:
  1. **Internal Sorting:** In this sorting technique, all the data is retained in main memory only and the data can be accessed randomly.
  2. **External sorting:** In this sorting, the data to be sorted is moved from secondary storage to main memory. Because the large data may be in secondary storage. It is more time consuming to move records into different location.

5.2.1 Definition

- We can define sorting as "arranging the data in either ascending or descending or alphabetically manner based on certain key in the record".

OR

- The process of arranging the data alphabetically or numerically is known as sorting.

5.2.2 Sorting Algorithms

- A sorting algorithm is a method that can be used to place a list of unordered items into an ordered sequence.

Efficiency of Sorting Algorithms:

- When comparing two different algorithms that solve the same problem, often one will be an order of magnitude more efficient than the other. In this case, it only makes sense that you be able to recognize and choose the more efficient algorithm.

- If a function is linear, i.e. if it contains no loops, then its efficiency is a function of the number of instructions it contains.
- In this case its efficiency is dependent on the speed of the computer and is generally not a factor in the overall efficiency in a program. On other hand, functions that loop will vary widely in their efficiency. The study of algorithm is devoted to the study of loops.
- The efficiency of algorithm is expressed as a function of the number of elements to be processed. The general format is F(n)=efficiency.

5.2.3 Classification Criteria of Sorting Algorithms

- Sorting algorithms used in computer science are often classified by:
    1. **Computational complexity:** (Worst, average and best behaviour) of elements comparisons in terms of size of the list. For typical sorting algorithms good behaviour is O(n log n) and worst behaviour is $O(n^2)$.
    2. **Memory usage (and use of other computer resources):** In particular, some sorting algorithms are "in place". This means that they need only O(1) memory beyond the items being sorted and they don't need to create auxiliary locations for data to be temporarily stored, as in the sorting algorithms.
    3. **Recursion:** Some algorithms are either recursive or non-recursive. Some other's may be both.
    4. **Stability:** Stable sorting algorithms maintain the relative order of records with equal keys.

5.3 Sorting Techniques (Oct. 2014)

- Sorting is the operation of arranging data or elements in some given order, numerically or alphabetically.
- The objective of sorting is to take an unordered set of comparable data items and arrange them in order.
- Various techniques of sorting are as shown in Fig. 5.1.

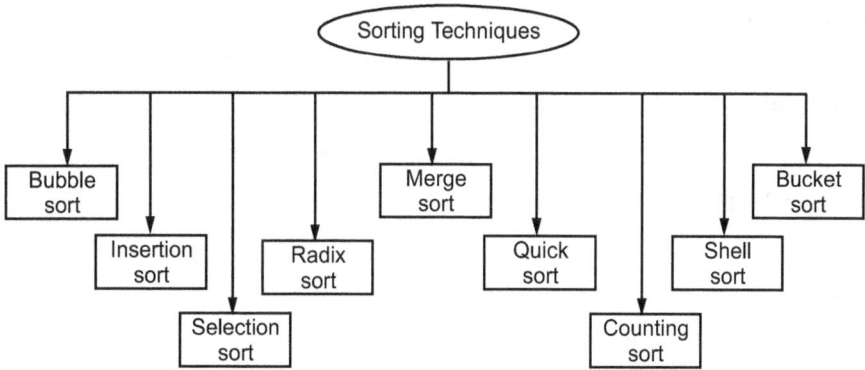

Fig. 5.1

5.3.1 Bubble Sort

- A bubble sort, also called a sinking sort or exchange sort. It is the oldest and simplest sort in use. It is used for sequencing small element lists.
- Bubble sort is one of the simple and most popular sorting method. It works by repeatedly stepping through the list to be sorted.
- Comparing each pair of adjacent items and swapping them if they are in wrong order.
- The bubble sort is the internal sorting type in which the smallest data item or elements are moved or "bubbled up" to the top.
- In this method, the first element is compared with the next element in the array.
- If the element is larger, then swap (exchange) them and move the smaller element (next) to the top position otherwise no exchange is required.
- After (n−1) comparisons, the largest element among all the elements will descends to the bottom of array.

Definition :

- A bubble sort, is a sorting algorithm that compares adjacent pairs and swaps them if necessary, causing the items to bubble up toward their proper position. The process continues until no swaps are necessary.

OR

- A sorting technique in which pairs of adjacent values in the list to be sorted are compared and interchanged if they are out of order; thus, list entries bubble upward in the list until they bump into one with a lower sort value.

Working of Bubble Sort:

- The bubble sort works by comparing each item in the list with the item next to it, and swapping them if required.
- The algorithm repeats this process until it makes a pass all the way through the list without swapping any items.
- This causes larger values to "bubble" to the end of the list while smaller values "sink" towards the beginning of the list.
- **Example :**

    Consider the array A is consist of following elements

40	20	70	10	92	54	62
0	1	2	3	4	5	6

Pass 1 :

1. 40 20 70 10 92 54 62
   Exchange (40 > 20)

2. 20 40 70 10 92 54 62
   No exchange

3. 20 40 70 10 92 54 62
   Exchange (70 > 10)

4. 20 40 10 70 92 54 62
   No Exchange

5. 20 40 10 70 92 54 62
   Exchange (92 > 54)

6. 20 40 10 70 54 92 62
   Exchange (92 > 62)

7. 20 40 10 70 54 62 |92|

- Now, we again do the some procedure to get sorted elements.

Pass 2 :

1. 20 40 10 70 54 62 |92|
   No Exchange

2. 20 40 10 70 54 62 |92|
   Exchange (40 > 10)

3. 20 10 40 70 54 62 |92|
   No Exchange

4. 20 10 40 70 54 62 |92|
   Exchange (70 > 54)

5. 20 10 40 54 70 62 92

Exchange (70 > 62)

6. 20 10 40 54 62 70 92

- We get list 20, 10, 40, 54, 62, 70, 92 but this is not sorted, so we can do the same procedure.

Pass 3 :

1. 20 10 40 54 62 70 92

Exchange (20 > 10)

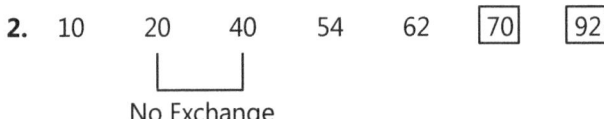

2. 10 20 40 54 62 70 92

No Exchange

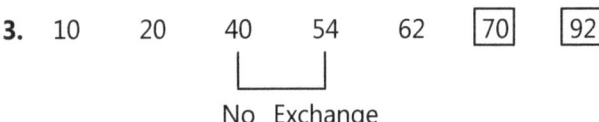

3. 10 20 40 54 62 70 92

No Exchange

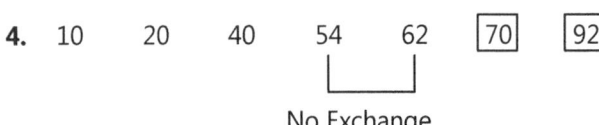

4. 10 20 40 54 62 70 92

No Exchange

5. 10 20 40 54 62 70 92

- This is our final sorted list. This is our final output.

Algorithm: Bubble Sort (A, N), where A is array and N is size.

    Step 1 : Start

    Step 2 : Accept N numbers.

    Step 3 : Repeat step 4 for i = 1 to N – 1 by 1.

    Step 4 : Repeat for j = 1 to N – i by 1

             if (A[j] > A[j + 1])

             Then swap A [j] with A[j + 1].

    Step 5 : Write sorted array.

    Step 6 : Stop.

Analysis and Complexity of Bubble Sort:

- A is an array consist of N numbers i.e. A[1] = A[i], A[2], A[3] .... A[N].
- Sorting the above elements means arranging the element in ascending or descending order.
- In this bubble sort algorithm, there are (n – 1) passes required.
- Each pass consists of comparing each element in the file with its successor i.e. A[i] with A[i + 1] and interchanging two elements if they are not in proper order.
- There are (n – 1) passes and (n – 1) comparisons on each pass. Thus, the total number of comparisons is

    $(n - 1) * (n - 1) = n^2 - 2n + 1$
    which is $o(n^2)$.
- It is comparison based sorting method. It is in place sorting method. It is adaptive sorting method as prestoredness affects the running time.

Advantages:
1. The primary advantage of the bubble sort is that it is popular and easy to implement.
2. In the bubble sort, elements are swapped in place without using additional temporary storage, so the space requirement is at a minimum.

Disadvantages:
1. The main disadvantage of the bubble sort is the fact that it does not deal well with a list containing a huge number of items.
2. The bubble sort is mostly suitable for academic teaching but not for real-life applications.
3. Very inefficient. General complexity is $O(n^2)$ while best case complexity is $O(n)$.

5.3.2 Selection Sort

- The selection sort algorithm starts by finding the minimum value in the array and moving it to the first position. This step is then repeated for the second lowest value, then the third, and so on until the array is sorted.

Working of Selection Sort:
- This is another popular method of sorting. In this, successive elements are selected in order and placed into their proper sorted position.
- In this the element, at first location is compared with further all elements in the list and exchange of element depends on the result of comparisons.
- With this after pass 1 the smallest element is at first position in the list.
- Similarly in the second pass the second lowest element will be located and placed at the 2nd position in the list.

- This process of locating and placing the smallest element at its proper position continues until all elements have been sorted in ascending order.
- Fig. 5.2 shows working of selection sort.

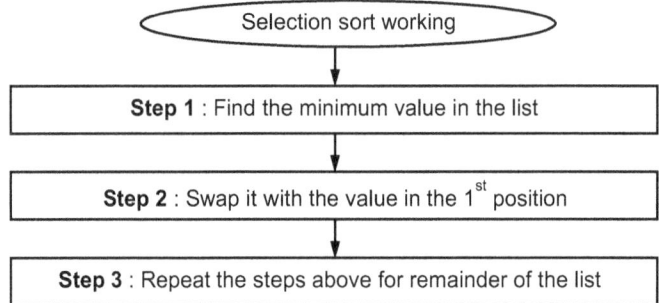

Fig. 5.2: Working of selection sort

- **Example :**

  Consider the array consist of following elements.

23	15	29	11	01	85	47
0	1	2	3	4	5	6

  Find the smallest element to place at first location.

Pass 1 :

|01| 15   29   11   23   85   47

Note : Actual swapping will take place at the end only after locating the smallest element.

Pass 2 : |01| |11| 29   15   23   85   47

Pass 3 : |01| |11| |15| 29   23   85   47

Pass 4 : |01| |11| |15| |23| 29   85   47

Pass 5 : |01| |11| |15| |23| |29| 85   47

Pass 6 : |01| |11| |15| |23| |29| |47| 85

Pass 7 : 01   11   15   23   29   47   85

Sorted List.

Algorithm: Selection sort (A, N), where, A is array and N is size.

    Step 1 : Start

    Step 2 : Accept N numbers

    Step 3 : Let pos = 0

    Step 4 : Find minimum in A, store in its position in s

    Step 5 : Swap A[pos] and A[s]

    Step 6 : pos = pos + 1

    Step 7 : Repeat 4, 5, 6, until pos <= 6

    Step 8 : Stop

Analysis and Complexity of Selection Sort:

- The performance of sorting algorithm depends upon the number of iterations and time to compare them.
- If there are n records or elements then (n – 1) comparisons are required.
- Thus, the total number of comparisons.

$$= (n-1) + (n-2) + (n-3) + \ldots + 1$$

$$= \frac{1}{2} n (n-1)$$

    which is $O(n^2)$

- Selection sort is less efficient on large lists than more advanced algorithms such as quick sort, heapsort or merge sort.
- It is simpler implementation, efficient for (quite) small data set, and not adaptive, and its stability depends on the implementation of choosing minimum.

Advantages:

1. The main advantage of the selection sort is that it performs well on a small list.
2. Furthermore, because it is an in-place sorting algorithm, no additional temporary storage is required beyond what is needed to hold the original list.

Disadvantage:

1. The primary disadvantage of the selection sort is its poor efficiency when dealing with a huge list of items.
2. The selection sort is only suitable for a list of few elements that are in random order.

5.3.3 Insertion Sort   (Oct. 2014)

- An insertion sort is a sorting method that sort a set of records by inserting records into an existing sorted array.
- The main purpose of insertion sort is to insert the element, in the ith pass in its right place.
- Insertion sort is a simple sorting algorithm that builds the final sorted array (or list) one item at a time.
- The insertion sort works just like its name suggests - it inserts each item into its proper place in the final list.

Working of Insertion Sort:

- In insertion sort, the first iteration starts with comparison of 1st element with the 0th element.
- In second iteration 2nd element is compared with the 0th and 1st element.
- In general in every iteration, an element is compared with all the elements.
- If at some point it is found that the element can be inserted at a position, then space is created for it by shifting the other elements one position to the right and inserting the element at the suitable position.
- This procedure is repeated for all the elements in the array.
- Insertion sort is more efficient than bubble sort because in insertion sort the element comparisons are less as compared to bubble sort.

Definition:

- A sorting algorithm that inserts each item in the proper place into an initially empty list by comparing it with each item in the list until it finds the new element's successor or the end of the list.

OR

- A simple sorting technique that scans the sorted list, starting at the beginning, for the correct insertion point for each of the items from the unsorted list.

Example : Consider the Array A consist of following elements.

24	56	47	36	11	91	85	32
0	1	2	3	4	5	6	7

Unsorted		Pass number (j)							Sorted
i	A[i]	1	2	3	4	5	6	7	8	8
0	24	24	24	24	24	11	11	11	11	11
1	56	56	56	47	36	24	24	24	24	24
2	47	47	47	56	47	36	36	36	32	32
3	36	36	36	36	56	47	47	47	36	36
4	11	11	11	11	11	56	56	56	47	47
5	91	91	91	91	91	91	91	85	56	56
6	85	85	85	85	85	85	85	91	85	85
7	32	32	32	32	32	32	32	32	91	91

Algorithm for Insertion sort :

Step 1 : Start.

Step 2 : Accept n numbers into array.

Step 3 : Data (0) is considered as a sorted file of one element.

Step 4 : Next = 1.

Step 5 : New element = data (next).

Step 6 : Move all elements by one position to the right.

Step 7 : Insert new element in the array at the position where step 5 terminated.

Step 8 : Next = Next + 1.

Step 9 : Continue from step 5 as long as next < n.

Step 10 : Stop.

Analysis and Complexity of Insertion Sort:

- If the file in this sort is sorted, only one comparison is made on each pass, so that complexity is O(n).
- If the file is this sort is initially sorted, then the complexity is $O(n^2)$. Since, the total number of comparison are given as $(n - 1) + (n - 2) + ... + 3 + 2 + 1 = (n - 1) * n/2$.
- Given complexity of this sort is $O(n^2)$ while best case is O(n).
- Simple implementation and efficient for (quite) small data sets.
- It is stable, it does not change relative order of elements with equal key.

Algorithm of Insertion Sort with Example:

Step 1 : Start

Step 2 : In this sorting, we compare each element with leftmost element. If left element is greater, then we do the swapping

For example, 24 56, 47, 36, 11, 91, 85, 32
↑

1. 24 < 56, Yes, so no swapping.
   24, 56, 47, 36, 11, 91, 85, 32
   ↑

2. 56 > 47, Yes, so swap we get
   24, 47, 56, 36, 11, 91, 85, 32
   ↑

3. 36 < 56, Yes, 36 < 47, yes, then swap and shift, we get
   24, 36, 47, 56, 11, 91, 85, 32
   ↑

4. 11 < 56 - Yes
   11 < 47 - Yes   then swap and shift, we get
   11 < 36 - Yes   11, 24, 36, 47, 56, 91, 85, 32
   11 < 24 - Yes   ↑

5. 91 < 56, no, then no exchange

6. 85 < 91, yes, then swap, we get
   11, 24, 36, 47, 56, 85, 91, 32

7. 32 < 91
   32 < 85
   32 < 56   Yes, then swap and shift, we get
   32 < 47   11, 24, 32, 36, 47, 56, 85, 91
   32 < 36

   This is our sorted list and final output.

Step 3 : Print the output (sorted list)

Step 4 : Stop

Advantages:

1. The main advantage of the insertion sort is its simplicity.
2. It also exhibits a good performance when dealing with a small list.
3. The insertion sort is an in-place sorting algorithm so the space requirement is minimal.

Disadvantages:
1. The disadvantage of the insertion sort is that it does not perform as well as other, better sorting algorithms.
2. The insertion sort is particularly useful only when sorting a list of few items.

5.3.4 Merge Sort

- In this method merging is a tool being used for sorting.
- Merging is the process of combining two sorted lists into single sorted list.
- To perform the merge sort both the sorted lists are compared. The smaller of both the element is stored in the third array. The sorting completes when all the elements from both the lists are placed into the third list.
- The basic idea of merge sort is:
  1. Divide the array to a number of sub-arrays.
  2. Sort each of these sub-arrays, and
  3. Merge them to get a single array.
- Merge sort is good for data that's too big to have in memory at once, because its pattern of storage access is very regular.
- It basically works on the principle of divide and conquer technique.
- In this method, first we divide the list into two sublists, with each sublist almost of equal sizes.
- Continues dividing the list will result in N sublist of size 1.
- Then merge adjacent pairs or arrays in a sorted way.

Definition:

- Merge sort is a sorting algorithm that sorts data items into ascending or descending order, which comes under the category of comparison-based sorting.

OR

- A sorting technique that sequences data by continuously merging items in the list. Every single item in the original unordered list is merged with another, creating groups of two. Every two-item group is merged, creating groups of four and so on until there is one ordered list.

Working of Merge Sort:

- The merge sort splits the list to be sorted into two equal halves, and places them in separate arrays. This sorting method is an example of the divide-and-conquer paradigm i.e. it breaks the data into two halves and then sorts the two half data sets recursively, and finally merges them to obtain the complete sorted list.

- The merge sort is a comparison sort and has an algorithmic complexity of O(n log n). Elementary implementations of the merge sort make use of two arrays - one for each half of the data set. Fig. 5.3 depicts the complete procedure of merge sort.

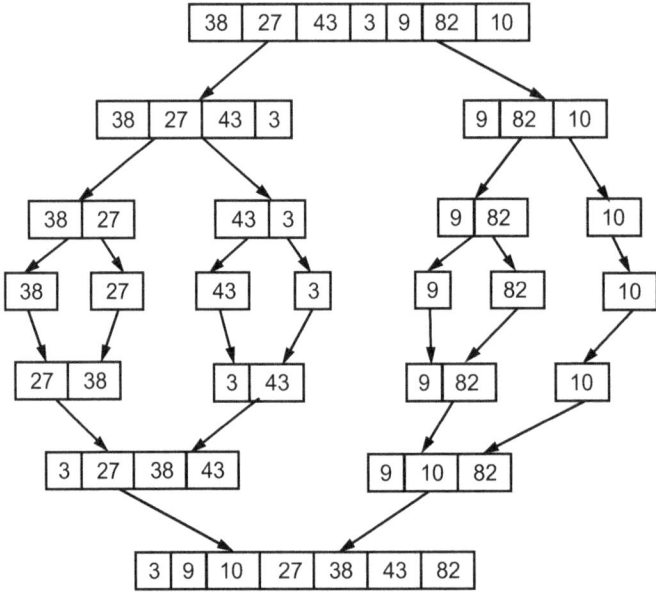

Fig. 5.3

For example:

- Consider an Array A with elements

    65   32   39   21   54   85   61   10   83   45

    Now break the list into two sublists

    First Sublist   65   32   39   21   54

    Second Sublist   85   61   10   83   45

    Again divide the two sublists

- Divide the array into n sublists of size 1. So we will have

- Now merge adjacent arrays, then we will have n/2 arrays of size 2. Repeat this process until one array remains of size n

| 21 | 32 | 39 | 65 | 10 | 54 | 61 | 85 | 45 | 83 |

| 10 | 21 | 32 | 39 | 54 | 61 | 65 | 85 | 45 | 83 |

| 10 | 21 | 32 | 39 | 45 | 54 | 61 | 65 | 83 | 85 |

- Hence the original Array A is sorted.

Algorithm for merge sort:
1. The arrays x and y are sorted using any of the discussed algorithms.
2. The 0th element from the first array1 is compared with 0th elements of second array2 since 0 < 1, 0 is moved in the third array.
3. Now 0th element of first array1 is compared with 1st element from second array2 since, 1 < 2 then 1 is moved in third array.
4. The same procedure is repeated till the end of the array is reached. Now the remaining elements from the other array are placed directly into the third list as are already in sorted order.

Complexity of Merge Sort:
- Its not adaptive. Merge sort is a stable sort as long as the merge operation is implemented properly.
- Not in-place sorting method, requires O(n) of additional memory space. The additional n locations were needed because one couldn't reasonably merge two sorted sets in place.

Advantages:
1. Good for sorting slow-access data (tape drive or hard disk).
2. It is excellent for sorting data that are normally accessed sequentially
3. Better at handling sequential-accessed lists.
4. If two equal valued items are in the list, then their relative locations are preserved (this is called sort-stable").
5. Marginally faster than the heap sort for larger sets.
6. Merge sort always does lesser number of comparisons than quick sort. Worst case for merge sort does about 39% less comparisons against quick sort's average case.

Disadvantages:
1. In many implementations, if the list is N long, then it needs 2 × N memory space to handle the sort.
2. If recursion is used to code the algorithm, then it uses twice as much stack memory as quick sort.

3. Its space complexity is very high. It requires about a O(n) auxiliary space for its working.
4. Function overhead calls (2n – 1) are much more than those for quick sort (n). This causes it to take more time marginally to sort the input data.

5.3.5 Radix Sort

- Radix sort is an algorithm that sorts a list of numbers and comes under the category of distribution sort.
- A radix sort is an algorithm that can rearrange integer representations based on the processing of individual digits in such a way that the integer representations are eventually in either ascending or descending order.
- Integer representations can be used to represent things such as strings of characters (names of people, places, things, the words and characters, dates, etc.) and floating point numbers as well as integers.
- So, anything which can be represented as an ordered sequence of integer representations can be rearranged to be in order by a radix sort.
- The radix sort is generally used when we intend to sort a large list of names alphabetically. Radix in this case can be 26, as there are 26 alphabets. If we want to arrange list of names we can classify names into 26 classes, where the first class consist of those names starting with 'A' and second class consist of names starting with 'B' and so on.
- Radix sort is an advanced method of sorting in which element are arranged in a sequential order.
- For numeric data or decimal numbers, there are 10 packets corresponding to the 10 decimal digits.
- In this technique, the number of iterations depends on the number of digits of the largest number in the list.
- In first iteration the list is sorted on the basis of the unit digit of the number.
- In the second pass, the 10 digits are sorted into packets.
- In the next iteration the 100 digits are sorted and so on.

Definition:

- An algorithm that puts data in order by classifying each item immediately rather than comparing it to other items.

OR

- Radix sort is a non-comparative integer sorting algorithm that sorts data with integer keys by grouping keys by the individual digits which share the same significant position and value.

Working of Radix Sort:

- This sorting algorithm doesn't compare the numbers but distributes them, it works as follows:

    1. Sorting takes place by distributing the list of number into a bucket by passing through the individual digits of a given number one-by-one beginning with the least significant part. Here, the number of buckets are a total of ten, which has key values starting from 0 to 9.

    2. After each pass, the numbers are collected from the buckets, keeping the numbers in order.

    3. Now, recursively redistribute the numbers as in the above step '1' but with a following reconsideration: take into account next most significant part of the number, which is then followed by above step '2'.

Classification:

- Radix sort can be classified as LSD (Least Significant Digit) radix sort process the integer representation starting from the least significant digit and move towards the most significant digit and MSD (Most Significant Digit) radix sorts use lexigraphic order, which is suitable for sorting strings, like fixed length integer representation or words.
- For example, consider the following sequence of numbers.

    242   986   428   143   312   101   090

Pass 1:

Input	Packets									
	0	1	2	3	4	5	6	7	8	9
242			242							
986							986			
428									428	
143				143						
312			312							
101		101								
090	090									

Pass 2: In this pass, ten's digit of a number are sorted.

Input	Packets									
	0	1	2	3	4	5	6	7	8	9
090										090
101	101									
242					242					
312		312								
143					143					
986									986	
428			428							

Pass 3: Here 100's digit of a number are sorted.

Input	Packets									
	0	1	2	3	4	5	6	7	8	9
101		101								
312				312						
428					428					
242			242							
143		143								
986										986
090	090									

- Now the array is sorted,
  090   101   143   242   312   428   986

Algorithm for Radix Sort:

1. In the first iteration, the elements are picked up and kept in various packets checking their unit's digit.
2. The cards are collected from packet 0 to packet 9 and again they are given as a input to the sorter.
3. In next iteration the ten's digits are sorted.
4. Repeat through step 2 until all digits end.

Analysis and Complexity of Radix Sort:

- Number of comparisons required for radix sort in worst case $f(n) = O(n^2)$ and in best case $f(n) = O(n \log n)$.

- The running time depends on the stable sort used as an intermediate stage of the sorting algorithm. When each digits is in the range 1 to k, and k is not too large, counting sort can be taken. In case of counting sort, each pass over n d-digit numbers takes O(n + k) time. There are d passes, so the total time for Radix sort is O(d(n+ k)). When d is constant and k = O(n), the Radix sort runs in linear time.

Advantages:
1. Radix sort is stable, preserving existing order of equal keys.
2. It works in linear time, unlike most other sorts. In other words, it do not bog down when large numbers of items need to be sorted.
3. The time to sort per item is constant, as no comparisons among items are made. With other sorts, the time to sort per time increases with the number of items.
4. Radix sort is particularly efficient when you have large numbers of records to sort with short keys.

Disadvantages:
1. Radix sort do not work well when keys are very long, as the total sorting time is proportional to key length and to the number of item to sort.
2. Radix sort is not "in-place", using more working memory than a traditional sort.
3. It takes more memory space than other sorting algorithms.

5.3.6 Shell Sort
- It is also called as a diminishing increment sort.
- Shell sort is superior method of sorting than bubble sort and insertion sort.
    1. This sorting method separates original array A into sub arrays each containing every k^{th} element of the original array.
    2. The k is called as an 'increment'. If k = 3, every sub array contains every third element. – sub array 1 contains element at position 0, 3, 6 and so on. Sub array 2 contains A[1], A[4].
    3. The first sub arrays are sorted mostly by simple insertion sort, then a new smaller value of k is chosen and the array is again partitioned and sorted.
    4. Ultimately, k becomes 1. Now at this stage, there is only one array containing all the elements which are in sorted order.
- **Example :**
  Data: 26, 58, 49, 38, 13, 93, 87, 34
  Suppose if k is chosen as 5, 3, 1 respectively, then

Iteration 1 : k = 5
Sub array
1. (A[0], A[5]) = (26, 93)
2. (A[1], A[6]) = (58, 87)
3. (A[2], A[7]) = (49, 34) $\Rightarrow$ (34, 49)
4. (A[3]) = (38)
5. (A[4]) = (13)

Iteration 1 : k = 5
    26   58   34   38   13   93   87   49

Iteration 2 : k = 3
Sub array
1. (A[0], A[3], A[6]) = (26, 38, 87)
2. (A[1], A[4], A[7]) = (58, 13, 49) => (13, 49, 58)
3. (A[2], A[5]) = (34, 93)

Iteration 2 : k = 3
    26   13   34   38   49   93   87   58

Iteration 3 : k = 1
(A[0], A[1], A[2], A[3], A[4], A[5], A[6], A[7])
DATA : 26, 13, 34, 38, 49, 93, 87, 58

Iteration 3 : k = 1
After iteration: 13   26   34   38   49   58   87   93

Now, we get a sorted array.

5.3.7 Quick Sort   (April 2015)

- Quick sort is one of the very popular sorting method. Quick sort follows divide and conquer strategy.
- The quick sort is a sorting algorithm, which is based on the divide and conquer principle, the steps for divide and conquer is given below for sorting a typical sub array A(p, q).
- The basic purpose of the quick sort is to move a data element (item) in the correct direction just enough for it to reach its final place in the array.
- It is also known as partition exchange sort.
- Quick sort is based on the divide and conquer paradigm, so it contains following process (take subarray A[p…r].
    1. **Divide:** The array A[p..r] is partitioned (rearranged) into two non-empty sub arrays A[p..q] and A[q + 1..r] such that each element of A[p..q] is less than or equal to each element of A[q + 1..r]. The index q is computed as part of this partitioning procedure.
    2. **Conquer:** The two sub arrays A[p..q] and A[q + 1..r] are sorted by recursive calls to quick sort.

3. **Combine:** Since the subarrays are sorted in place, no work is needed to combine them, the entire array A[p..r] is now sorted.

Definition:

- A sorting technique that sequences a list by continuously dividing the list into two parts and moving the lower items to one side and the higher items to the other.

OR

- A sorting algorithm that operates by recursively partitioning the items to be sorted into two sets.

Working of Quick Sort:

- Quick sort is an algorithm based on the divide-and-conquer paradigm that selects a pivot element and reorders the given list in such a way that all elements smaller to it are on one side and those bigger than it are on the other.
- Then the sub lists are recursively sorted until the list gets completely sorted. The time complexity of this algorithm is O (n log n).

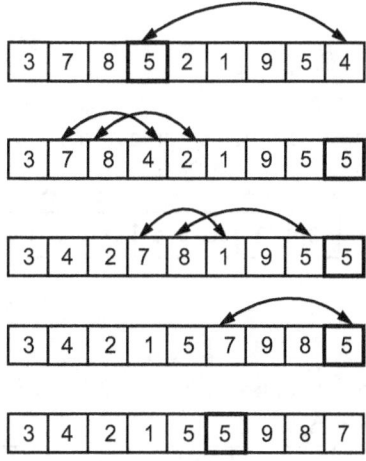

The following function implements the quick sort. Quick sort (A, p, r).

Step 1 : Start
Step 2 : If (p < r) then
    q = partition (A, p, r)
Step 3 : quick sort (A, p, q)
Step 4 : quick sort (A, q + 1, r)
Step 5 : Stop

- We are not bound to the choice of the first item in the list as the pivot; we can choose any item we wish and swap it. With the first item before beginning the loop that partitions the list. In fact first item is often a poor choice for pivot.

- Since if the list is already sorted, then the first key will have not other less than it, and so one of the sublist will be empty. Hence let us instead choose a pivot near the centre of the list, in the hope that our choice will partition the keys so that about half come on each side of the pivot.

Partitioning an array:

The key to the algorithm is the PARTITION function, which rearranges the subarray A[p..r] in place.

Partition (A, p, r):

Step 1 : x = A[p], i = p – 1, j = r + 1.
Step 2 : As long as A [j], ≤ x, j = j – 1,
Step 3 : Increment 'i' value as long as
A [i] ≥ x.
Step 4 : If (i < j) then
swap A [i] and A [j]
else return j.
Step 5 : If (i < j) then step 2.
Step 6 : Stop.

Fig. 5.4 show operation of partition on a sample array.

A [p...r]

| 5 | 3 | 2 | 6 | 4 | 1 | 3 | 7 |

↑   ↑
i   j

Fig. 5.4

(a) The input array, with the initial values of 'i' and 'j' just off the left and right ends of the array. We partition around x = A[p] = 5

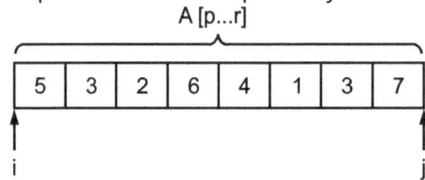

(b) The positions of i and j at step 4 of first iteration.

| 3 | 3 | 2 | 6 | 4 | 1 | 5 | 7 |

↑   ↑
i   j

(c) The result of exchanging the elements pointed to by i and j in step 4.

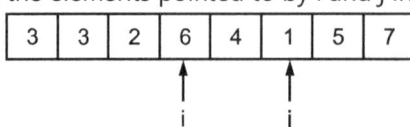

(d) The position of i and j at step 4, of second iteration.

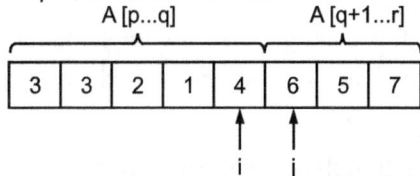

(e) The position of i and j at step 4, at third iteration. The function terminates because 'i' ≥ 'j' the value q = j is returned. The array elements upto, including A[j] are less than or equal to x = 5, and those after A[j] are greater than or equal to x = 5.

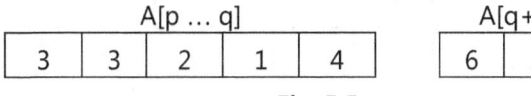

Fig. 5.5

Example: Sort the numbers 25, 57, 48, 37, 12, 92, 86, 03. The execution of quick sort is shown below.

```
Sort (25, 57, 48, 37, 12, 92, 86, 03)
    pivot : 25; partition into (12, 03) and (57, 48, 37, 92, 86)
        Sort (12, 03)
        Pivot : 12, partition into (03) and (NIL)
            Sort (03)
            Sort (NIL)
            Combine into (03, 12)

        Sort (57, 48, 37, 92, 86
        Pivot : 57, partition into (48, 37) and (92, 86)
            Sort (48, 37)
            Pivot : 48, partition into (37) and (NIL)
            Sort (37)
            Sort (NIL)
                Combine into (37, 48)

            Sort (92, 86)
            Pivot : 92, partition into (86) and (NIL)
            Sort (86)
            Sort (NIL)
            Combine into (86, 92)

        Combine into 37, 48, 57, 86, 92
    Combine into 03, 12, 25, 37, 48, 57, 86, 92.
```

Analysis of Complexity of Quick Sort:

- Auxiliary space used in the average case for implementing recursive function calls is O (log n) and hence proves to be a bit space costly, especially when it comes to large data sets.
- Its worst case has a time complexity of $O(n^2)$ which can prove very fatal for large data sets. Competitive sorting algorithms.
- A graphical plot of the time complexity of the Quick Sort gives a pictorial overview about the efficiency of the algorithm. The plot is as shown in Fig. 5.6.

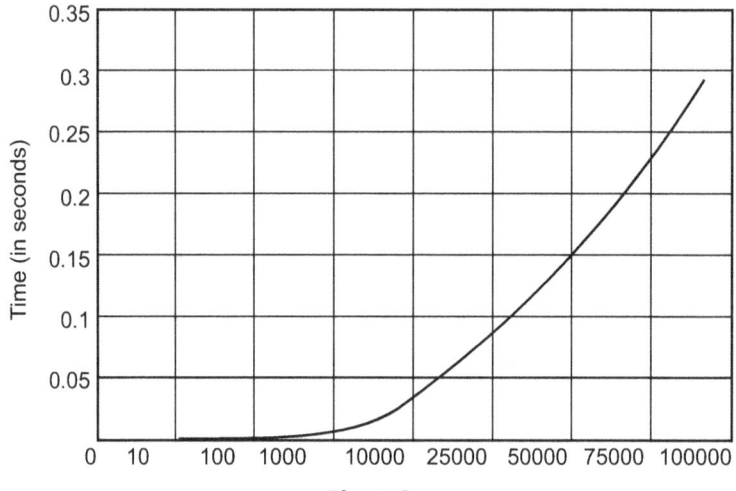

Fig. 5.6

- The known fastest in place algorithm in practices. Each call finalises the correct position of pivot element which can never be changed by any subsequent calls.
- It is an adaptive sorting method.

Advantages

1. Quick sort is an in-place sort that needs no temporary memory.
2. Typically, quick sort is faster in practice than other algorithms, because its inner loop can be efficiently implemented on most architectures.
3. In most real-world data, it is possible to make design choices which minimize the probability of requiring quadratic time.
4. Quick sort tends to make excellent usage of the memory hierarchy like virtual memory or caches. It is well suited to modern computer architectures.
5. Quick sort can be easily parallelised due to its divide-and-conquer nature.

Disadvantages:

1. This algorithm may swap the elements with equal comparison keys (it is not a stable sort).

2. Simpler algorithms like insertion sort perform better for the small (10 elements or about) data sets. The advanced implementations automatically switch into simpler alternative algorithm if the data set is small enough.
3. Quick sort does not work very well on already mostly sorted lists or on lists with lot of similar values.

5.3.8 Counting Sort

- A sorting technique that is used when the range of keys is relatively small and there are duplicate keys. Counting sorts differ from sorts that compare data in multiple passes.
- They work by creating an array of counters the size of the largest integer in the list; therefore, the keys must be integers or data that can be readily converted to integers.
- Counting sort is an algorithm used to sort data whose range is pre-specified and multiple occurrences of the data are encountered. It is possibly the simplest sorting algorithm.
- The essential requirement is that the range of the data set from which the elements to be sorted are drawn, is small compared to the size of the data set.

| 3 | 1 | 4 | 1 | 5 | 9 | 2 | 6 | 5 | 4 | Data |

| 0 | 2 | 1 | 1 | 2 | 2 | 1 | 0 | 0 | 1 | Counts |
| 0 | 1 | 2 | 3 | 4 | 5 | 6 | 7 | 8 | 9 | |

Fig. 5.7

Modify the counting array we get,

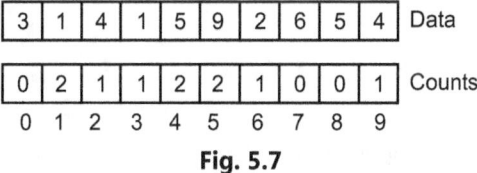

We get,

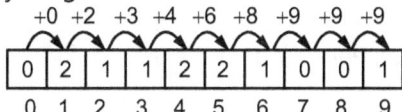

Now, remove last element from array A. (i.e. 4). Find the value at index position '4' in the counts array, which is 6. Therefore, add '4' at the sixth position in the output array B. Also, the value at position '4' in counts array become 6 − 1 = 5. Now, consider, second last element, i.e. 5. The value at 5th index position i.e. counts [5] = 8. Add '5' in the 8th position in array B. Update counts [5] = 8 − 1 = 7.

Repeat this procedure till the removal of the first element i.e. 3. The output array 'B' is as follows.

| 1 | 1 | 2 | 3 | 4 | 4 | 5 | 5 | 6 | 9 |

The counts array after updation is given below.

| 0 | 0 | 2 | 3 | 4 | 6 | 8 | 9 | 9 | 9 |
| 0 | 1 | 2 | 3 | 4 | 5 | 6 | 7 | 8 | 9 |

Definition:
- Counting sort is an algorithm for sorting a collection of objects according to keys that are small integers; that is, it is an integer sorting algorithm.
- A sort algorithm not based on comparisons and supports duplicate keys.
- Most of the algorithms cannot do better than O(n log n). This algorithm assumes that each input element is in the range 0 to k for some integer k. The basic idea is to determine for each input element x, the number of elements less than x.
- This information is used to place the element x directly into its position in the output array.

A is an input array of length n
B is the output array.
C is an auxiliary array of size k.

Assumption: A consists of elements with integer keys in the range [1..k]

Counting-Sort (A, B, k)
For i ← 1 to k
C[i] ← = 0
for j ← 1 to n
C[A[j]] ← C[A[j]] + 1
// C[i] = the number of appearances of i in A.
for i ← 2 to k
C[i] ← C[i] + C[i-1]
// C[i] = the number of elements in A that are ≤ i
for j ← n downto 1
B[C[A[j]]] ← A[j]
C[A[j]] ← C[A[j]] - 1
return B

Run-time Complexity: O(n+k)
- This is an improvement on comparison-based sorts, which need n*logn time.
- Counting sort is stable, two elements with the same key value will appear in the output in the same order as they appeared in the input.

Stability is important when there is additional data besides the key.

Analysis and Complexity of Counting Sort:
- The algorithm has a time complexity of O(n + k), where n is the number of data while k is the range of the data, which implies that the most efficient use will be when k<<n. In that case the time complexity will turn out to be linear.
- The loop of lines 1-2 takes O(k) time.
- The loop of lines 3-4 takes O(n) time.

- The loop of lines 6-7 takes O(k) time.
- The loop of lines 9-11 takes O(n) time.
- Therefore, the overall time of the counting sort is O(k) + O(n) + O(k) + O(n) = O(k + n)
- In practice, we usually use counting sort algorithm when have k = O(n), in which case running time is O(n).
- The Counting sort is a stable sort i.e., multiple keys with the same value are placed in the sorted array in the same order that they appear in the input array.

5.3.9 Bucket Sort

- Bucket sort is a sorting method that subdivides the given data into various buckets depending on certain characteristic order, thus partially sorting them in the first go. Then depending on the number of entities in each bucket, it employs either bucket sort again or some other ad hoc sort.
- Bucket sort runs in linear time on an average. It assumes that the input is generated by a random process that distributes elements uniformly over the interval 1 to m.
- Bucket sort is categorized into linear time sorting algorithms. In bucket sort, no comparisons needed between elements. But it depends on assumption about the numbers being sorted.
- Bucket sort takes input as *n* real numbers in the range of 0 and 1. Basic idea of bucket sort is that it create *n* linked lists (*buckets*) to divide interval [0,1) into subintervals of size 1/*n*. Then it adds each input element to appropriate bucket and sort buckets with insertion sort. Uniform input distribution is O(1) bucket size. Therefore the expected total time is O(n).

    Bucket sort works as follows:
    1. Set up an array of initially empty "buckets".
    2. **Scatter:** Go over the original array, putting each object in its bucket.
    3. Sort each non-empty bucket.
    4. **Gather:** Visit the buckets in order and put all elements back into the original array.

Definition of Bucket Sort:

- It is referred to a variety of sorting techniques that reserve an array of fields in memory (buckets), the number of which is based on the values in the key being sorted

OR

- Bucket sort, or bin sort, is a sorting algorithm that works by partitioning an array into a number of buckets. Each bucket is then sorted individually, either using a different sorting algorithm, or by recursively applying the bucket sorting algorithm.

Bucket Sort Algorithm

```
Bucket Sort( array A, int n, int M)
    {
       for i = 1 to M
       {
           bin[i]   = Empty
       }
       for i  = 1 to n
       {
           bin[A[i]] = A[i]
       }
    }
```

Example of Bucket Sort:
Step 1:

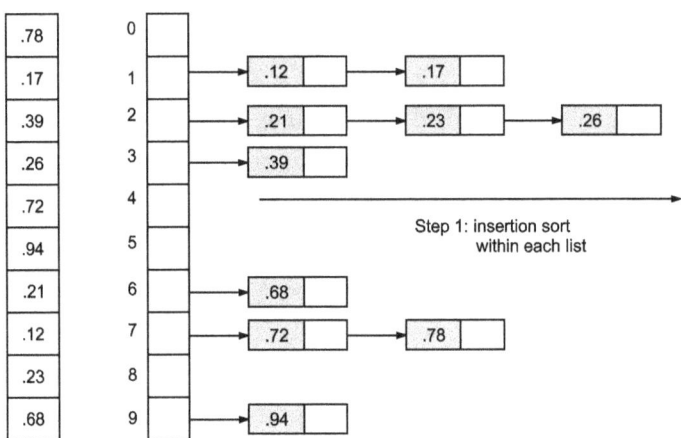

Step 1: insertion sort within each list

Step 2:

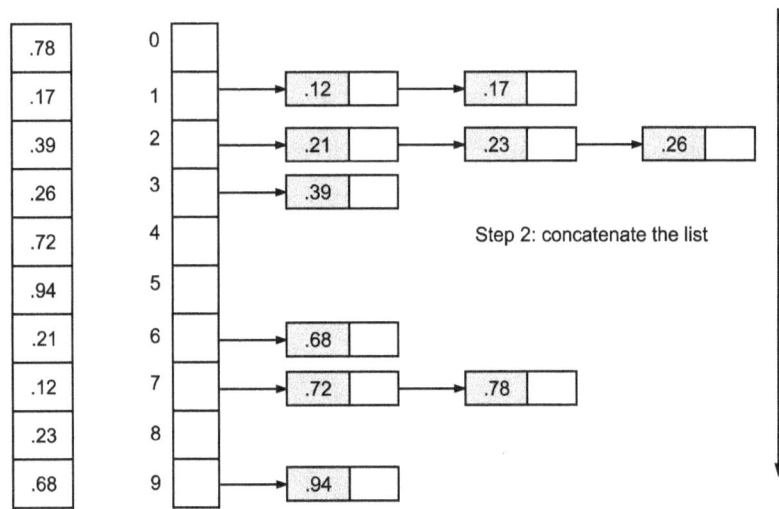

Step 2: concatenate the list

Step 3:

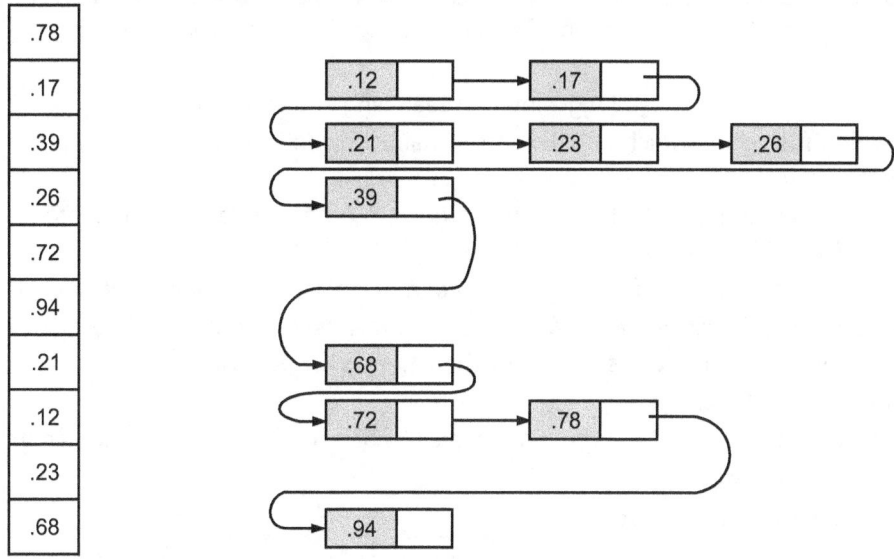

Analysis and Complexity of Bucket Sort:

- This is because the comparisons are being done n times at each of the 'd' levels that the data has to pass before getting sorted. Thus, the overall complexity is nd.
- Thus we can mathematically derive that if n.d < n log n, then

  d< log n => log (range) < log n => range<=n

Advantage:

1. Bucket sort is an example of a sorting algorithm that runs in O(n). This is possible only because Bucket sort does not rely primarily on comparisons in order to perform sorting.

Disadvantages:

1. Bucket sort is not useful when scanning the buckets for large arrays which is too costly.
2. For a non-uniform distribution this sort fails to be so efficient because the empty buckets would unnecessarily cause slow down.

Comparison of Sorting Methods:

Name	Time Complexity			Space Complexity
	Best	Average	Worst	
Bubble sort	O(n)	O(n^2)	O(n^2)	O(n)
Insertion sort	O(n)	O(n^2)	O(n^2)	O(n)
Selection sort	O(n^2)	O(n^2)	O(n^2)	O(n)
Quick sort	O(n log n)	O(n log n)	O(n^2)	O(n log n)
Merge sort	O(n log n)	O(n log n)	O(n log n)	O(2n)

5.4 Searching (April 2015)

- Searching refers to the operation of finding the location of a given item in a collection of items.
- There are two types of searching - internal searching and external searching.
- Searching method in which all elements remain constantly in own memory are called as 'internal search'.
- Searching method in which elements are kept on secondary storage are called as 'external search'.
- Searching is the process of finding the location of a given element in a set of elements.
- The search is said to be successful if the given element is found i.e., the element does exist in the collection such as an array; otherwise it is unsuccessful.

Definition of Searching:
- The process of locating the target data in a collection of items is known as searching.

Types of Searching:
- Fig. 5.8 shows types of searching.

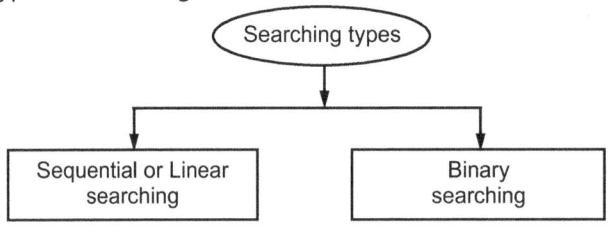

Fig. 5.8

1. **Linear search:**
- This method traverses a list sequentially to locate the search key.
- Linear search also referred as sequential search, is the simplest searching technique.
- The search begins at one end of the list and searches for the required element one by one until the element is found or till the end of the list is reached.
- The search is said to be successful if the element is found and unsuccessful if the search element is not found in the list.
- The linear search technique does not require that items in the list are to be in sorted order.

2. **Binary search:**
- This method works on sorted lists by progressively making better guesses to find the location of a search key.
- The binary search algorithm is one of the most efficient searching techniques, which requires the list to be sorted in ascending order.
- To search for an element in the list, the binary search algorithm splits the list and locates the middle elements of the list. It is then compared with the search element. If the search element is less than the middle element, the first part of the list is searched else the second part of the list is searched.

- The algorithm again reduces the list into two halves, locates the middle element and compares with the search element. If the search element is less than the middle element, the first part of the list is searched.
- The process continues until the search element is equal to the middle element or the list consists of only one element that is not equal to the search element.

5.4.1 Linear Search   (Oct. 2014)
- Linear search is the easiest search technique in which each element is scanned in a sequential manner to locate the desired element.
- In this method, search begins with the first available record and proceeds to the next available record until we find the target key or conclude that it is not found. Linear search is also called as 'sequential search'.

5.4.1.1 Definition
- Linear search, also known as sequential search, is a process that checks every element in the list sequentially until the desired element is found.

OR

- Linear search or sequential search is a method for finding a particular value in a list, that consists of checking every one of its elements, one at a time and in sequence, until the desired one is found.
- **Example:** Consider an array with 5 elements

3	21	11	91	19
0	1	2	3	4

- We are searching for element 91. To search 91 the item 91 is compared with element at A[0] then A[1] and so on. Until we find the target value or reach to the end of array.
- When item is found it displays the location of an item else displays item not found.

Algorithm:
    Step 1 : Start
    Step 2 : Accept n values from user i.e. array elements.
    Step 3 : Accept element to be searched from user i.e. target.
    Step 4 : Set i = 0, flag = 0
    Step 5 : Compare A[i] with target
        if (A[i]=target)
            set flag = 1 goto step 7
        else
            move to next data element
                i = i + 1;
    Step 6 : If (i < = n) go to step 5
    Step 7 : If (flag = 1) then
            Return i as position of target located use.
            Else
            Otherwise report as target not found.
    Step 8 : Stop.

Analysis and Complexity of Linear Search:

- For a list with n items, the best case is when the value is equal to the first element of the list, in which case only one comparison is needed. The worst case is when the value is not in the list (or occurs only once at the end of the list), in which case n comparisons are needed.
- If the value being sought occurs k times in the list, and all orderings of the list are equally likely, the expected number of comparisons is, if the value being sought occurs once in the list, and all orderings of the list are equally likely, the expected number of comparisons is $\frac{n+1}{2}$. However, if it is known that it occurs once, than at most n − 1 comparisons are needed, and the expected number of comparisons is (for example, for n = 2 this is 1, corresponding to a single if-then-else construct).
- Either way, asymptotically the worst-case cost and the expected cost of linear search are both O(n).

5.4.1.2 Advantages and Disadvantages

Advantages:

1. A simple and easy method.
2. Better to use for unsorted data.
3. Suitable for storage structure, which do not support direct access to data.
4. The primary advantage of linear search is its simplicity; conceptually, it's extraordinarily easy to understand, and, implementation-wise, it's also very straight-forward.
5. From an operational standpoint, linear search also is very resource efficient - it does not require copying/partitioning of the array being search, and thus is memory-efficient.
6. It also operates equally well on both unsorted and sorted data.

Disadvantages:

1. Linear search efficient for only small list.
2. Highly inefficient for large data.
3. The primary disadvantage of linear search is that it has a very poor O(n) general efficiency.
4. The performance of the algorithm scales linearly with the size of the input.
5. Linear search is slower than many other search algorithms.
6. Performance of this method degrades, when the list grows.

5.4.2 Binary Search (Oct. 2014, April 2015)

- Linear search is not suitable for longer lists as it required N comparisons in worst case. There is a technique which is very fast and efficient than Linear search called as 'binary search'.
- It requires list of elements in a sorted manner either ascending or descending.
- Binary search algorithm uses the divide and conquer method to search the list.

5.4.2.1 Definition

- A technique for quickly locating an item in a sequential list. The desired key is compared to the data in the middle of a sequential index or in the middle of a sequential file. The half that contains the data is then compared in the middle, and so on, either until the key is located or a small enough group is isolated to be sequentially searched.

OR

- Binary search method employs the process of searching for a record only in half of the list, depending on the comparison between the element to be searched and the central element in the list.
- In this searching method, the list's centre element is calculated with formula:

    MID = (BEG + END)/2

    after calculating the mid value the item to be searched is compared with the element present at mid value.
- If it matches the search is successful otherwise the list is divided into two halves.
    (i) First, from 0th element to the centre element (first half).
    (ii) Second, from centre element to the last element (second half).
- As a result all the elements in the first half are smaller than the centre element and all the elements in the second half are greater than the centre element.
- Now check whether target element is greater or smaller than the centre element.
- If element is smaller than centre element searching is done in first half otherwise it is in second half and process is continued.

Example :

Array [7]	=	{	3,	15,	19,	23,	45,	71,	90	}
			1	2	3	4	5	6	7	

item = 15

1.   BEG = 1 END = 7

        MID = (BEG + END) / 2 i.e. (1 + 7) / 2

      Array [MID] = Array[4] = 23

                    Array [MID] > Item   i.e. (23 > 15)
                        END = MID – 1
                              = 4 – 1
                              = 3
   2.   BEG = 1   END = 3
                        MID = (1 + 3)/2
                              = 2
                    Array [MID] = Array[2] = 15
        "Item 15 found at location 2"

Algorithm:
  Step 1: Start
  Step 2: Let n be the size of the list let target be the element to search. Let flag = 0 BEG = 1 END = n.
  Step 3: If (BEG < = END) then MID = (BEG + END)/2 else goto step 5.
  Step 4: If (Array[MID] = target) then
              POS = MID, flag = 1 and
              goto step 5.
        else
              if (Array[MID] > target)
                  END = MID – 1
              else
                  BEG = MID + 1;
  Step 5: Goto step 3
  Step 6: If flag = 1
              Report element found at location "pos"
        else
              Report element not found in the list
  Step 7: Stop

Analysis and Complexity of Binary Search:
- Binary search can be analyzed with the best, worst, and average case number of comparisons. This analysis is dependent upon the length of the array, so let N = [A] denote the length of the Array A.
- The numbers of comparisons for the recursive and iterative versions of binary search are the same, if comparison counting is relaxed slightly. For recursive binary search, count each pass through the if-then-else block as one comparison. For Iterative binary search, count each pass through the while block as one comparison. Best case O(1) comparisons.
- In the best case, the item X is the middle in the array A. A constant number of comparisons (actually just 1) are required. Worst case O (log n) comparisons.
- In the worst case, the item X does not exist in the array A at all. Through each recursion or iteration of binary search, the size of the admissible range is halved.

5.4.2.2 Advantages and Disadvantages

Advantages:
1. Suitable for sorted data.
2. Efficient for large list.
3. Suitable for storage structure that support direct access.
4. Very fast method as compare to linear search.
5. It needs fewer comparisons.

Disadvantages:
1. Not suitable for unsorted data.
2. This method is inefficient for small lists.
3. Expensive method because it requires data in sorted order.

Comparison of Linear and Binary Search: (Oct. 2014, April 2015)

Binary Search	Linear Search
1. This method search in left or right sublist by comparing element with middle element of array..	1. In this method, searching in linear fashion w.r.t. key.
2. This is faster method.	2. Slower than binary search.
3. This search method is used for only one dimensional array.	3. This search method is used for single as well as multidimensional array.
4. In binary search data should be in sorted order.	4. In linear search data can be in sorted or unsorted order.

Questions

1. What is searching?
2. Define sorting.
3. Describe the bubble sort with suitable example.
4. Explain the term efficiency of sorting algorithm in detail.
5. Describe binary search with example.
6. Explain the following sorting techniques with examples.
    (i) Shell sort
    (ii) Radix sort
    (iii) Quick sort

7. What are the advantages of selection sort.
8. Explain linear search with example.
9. Compare linear and binary search techniques.
10. Enlist advantages and disadvantages of bubble sort.
11. With suitable example describe selection sort.
12. What is counting sort? Explain with example. Also state its advantages and disadvantages.
13. With the help of example describe bucket sort in detail.

University Questions and Answers

October 2014

1. What is sequential search? [2M]
   Ans. Please refer to Section 5.4.1.
2. List sorting techniques. [2M]
   Ans. Please refer to Section 5.3 .
3. Explain concept of insertion sort with example. [4M]
   Ans. Please refer to Section 5.3.3.
4. Write an algorithm for Binary Search. [4M]
   Ans. Please refer to Section 5.4.2.
5. Compare linear and binary search. [4M]
   Ans. Please refer to Page 5.35.

Summer 2015

1. List searching techniques. [2M]
   Ans. Please refer to Section 5.4.
2. Explain Binary Search with example. [4M]
   Ans. Please refer to Section 5.4.2.
3. Explain quick sort with example. [4M]
   Ans. Please refer to Section 5.3.7.
4. Compare Linear search and binary search. [4M]
   Ans. Please refer to Page 5.35.

***

www.ingramcontent.com/pod-product-compliance
Lightning Source LLC
Chambersburg PA
CBHW080052190426
43201CB00035B/2271